DIMINUTIVE DRAMAS

DIMINUTIVE DRAMAS

BY

MAURICE BARING

⋯

ONE-ACT PLAYS IN REPRINT

Core Collection Books, inc.

GREAT NECK, NEW YORK

First Edition 1910
Fourth Edition 1938
Reprinted 1977

INTERNATIONAL STANDARD BOOK NUMBER
0-8486-2012-7

LIBRARY OF CONGRESS CATALOG NUMBER
77-70343

PRINTED IN THE UNITED STATES OF AMERICA

DEDICATED TO

A. I.

WHOSE UNWRITTEN CHRONICLES ARE BETTER
THAN BOOKS AND WHOSE UNPREMEDITATED
SUGGESTION HITS A TARGET BEYOND
THE REACH OF ARTISTS AND THE
KEN OF CRITICS

These "Diminutive Dramas" first appeared in the *Morning Post*, and are reprinted here by the courtesy of the Editor.

The Acting Rights are reserved.

Application for permission to perform any of the plays contained in this volume should be addressed to—

The Secretary,

The Incorporated Society of Authors,

Playwrights and Composers,

11, Gower St., London, W.C. 1.

No performances may be given except under licence from the Society named.

PREFACE

W. S. GILBERT, in one of the best poems in the English
language, wrote, with regard to the apparition of a Red
Indian at the gate of a Turkish house:—

> To say that Ahmed ope'd his eyes
> Would faintly paint his great surprise.
> To say it nearly made him die
> Would be to paint it much too high.

That is what Gilbert wrote, as well as I can remember
after nearly fifty years, and if I have got it wrong by
a word or two, that doesn't much matter; for I have
noticed that when people change a text through
quoting from memory they usually change it for the
better.

Anyhow, this immortal quatrain is suitable to what
I have here to say. When I first heard that Mr. Baring's
Trilogy was at last to be bound up in one volume I
cried out of my own accord, "The desire of the everlasting hills has come." The words are not my own
but the emotion I think is. I now see that the
emotion in cold print looks exaggerated. Either
Talleyrand or somebody else said that whatever is
exaggerated is worthless, and in saying so said something quite untrue. Still, exaggeration does take away
from the value of a statement.

On the other hand were I to say of the appearance of this book that it gave me peculiar satisfaction it would be to paint my feelings much too low.

Its appearance marks a day in my life. For years I have been praying in secret, canvassing in private and crying aloud in public that it was a duty to English letters to print these three masterpieces between two covers and to issue them as one book. There is thus an exact blend of savours for there is a subtle difference between the letters and the diaries, between the diaries and the letters and the dramas. Nor does it matter very much in what order you read them for they form not a sequence but a ring. Until they appeared as one book men knew some one or some other but not the whole. Now they will be known together and will achieve a permanence which they do not so much deserve as obtain of right.

There are now three books which stand out separate from the rest of the English prose work done in my lifetime. These three books are The Diary of a Nobody, The Wallet of Kai-Lung and this collection here before you. In each the character is that of a genus: a separate category. For it is true of these books as of angels. (Each angel we are told by those scholars who have studied the affair has a separate nature from every other angel. The angels are not in a lump but individual, differing one from another as much as an elephant does from a flea.) So it is with The Diary of a Nobody, so it is with The Wallet of Kai-Lung, and so it is with the present work. *Opus magnum et perdurabile.*

The Diary of a Nobody is the essence of the nation. The Wallet of Kai-Lung the essence of ironic wisdom, but this Trilogy of Mr. Baring's is something of yet another kind. It is the essence of what is civilised. It is the only thing in modern English letters which is wholly European and classic.

Here again I shall be told I have fallen over the edge into exaggeration. I don't think so myself but what a man thinks of his own opinion, of his own rooted opinion at least, is of no moment to his readers. What is of moment to his readers is what they think of his opinion. So if my readers think that the word "only" is an exaggeration, I will bow to them and leave it out. I will confine myself to saying that this book is, unlike the other two triumphs, European and classic; and that they may, my readers that is, go out to search for something else which shall be European and classic in modern English Letters. They will not find it.

The first mark, the chief test, of such a character in anything—a statue, an epigram, a life, a story—is economy: that is, the use of your material to its best effect: the making of it pull every ounce of its weight.

Look at a Greek marble head, or better still at the best Egyptian granite. Look at that great forearm and fist which are the glory of the British Museum and see with what excision of superfluity the thing is done. It is not a suggestion of beauty in the one case or of strength in the other: it is not an impression, or a hint, or an outline: it is the thing itself. By economy you get the soul of the thing. After seeing a work of art dependent for its triumph upon economy then the real thing of which it is an imitation, seems, by contrast, to be marred by too much detail. It seems to have less unity, to be less itself.

Read carefully the words used by Calypso to Mercury and then to Ulysses and you will see what I mean. Or again read Clytemnestra's letters in their order and observe the gradation. Then ask yourself how it is done. That is economy.

There is another way of putting it. If an enemy should desire to spoil Mr. Baring's book for posterity and render it worthless he would only have to go over it with the help of a commonplace mind and put in at every turn the redundant words which he himself would have written.

It is not only the exactitude of the terms the writer uses nor the order in which he puts them, it is also the numerical value of the total which counts; and this, in the case of words is the exact opposite of what it is in the case of money. The more sovereigns you give me, in the days when an angry people shall demand and obtain gold again, the better shall I be pleased. But the less words you give me, the better shall I be pleased also.

This is not to say that mere paucity of words is of value. There are fools who talk like that in universities. They are not all dead yet. But it is to say that, effect for effect, a similar effect with less words is stronger than one with more words, and, one with the least number of words necessary for the full statement bears the greatest weight.

It is not to say either that rhetoric or exuberance demand this restriction. With them it is the other way about. The repetitions of the Psalter, the cascades of Rabelais, depend for their value on verbal largesse. Yet even here there is economy in execution. For writing of that sort is only possible either because the writer has such a store that he will never overlap nor make two words do the work of one, or because his repetitions are calculated.

But though economy is the first mark of the writing

to which these lines form a paltry introduction there is a great deal more.

There is wit, acting as wit should, by simplicity and implication without trick or aid of any kind.

It is wit and not humour. Humour is founded upon folly but wit is founded upon reason; and where the reason works upon exact and multiple observation, upon the knowledge of men and things, there you get wit boiled down to its greatest strength, like a double consommé.

Wit is at its highest in Mr. Baring's work where he gives us the conversation or correspondence of the leisured woman. But it is present everywhere. It is present when he is laughing at his subject or when his subject is laughing at you. It is present in the remark of Lucullus about the dish of larks' tongues and it is present in the amiable simplicity of the Greek traveller reporting current talk about the Emperor. It is present perhaps at its best in the letter of King Lear's daughter.

But I do not very much believe in grading unsurpassed work and giving higher marks to this than to that in such a collection as the one now before me. Mere serial arrangement of that kind ignores quality. It tends to propose comparison between things which cannot be compared. But if one goes by what has most moved oneself I do feel the letter about King Lear's visit more even than I feel the banquet, the public banquet, at Puteoli.

Well there it is. I will not go on writing, for criticism is not my trade; nor writing either, for that matter. I have been compelled to take to writing from early youth as a drowning dog with a brick round its neck is compelled to treading water; but I was never born for it. Give me rather enjoyment, satisfaction, happiness;

which is the true end of man. And this Trilogy will always make me happy and after I am dead it will make happy I know not how many yet unborn.

As for those who do not understand what I mean, let them perish for what they are: deaf, dumb and blind.

H. BELLOC.

King's Land.
January, 1935.

CONTENTS

DIMINUTIVE DRAMAS

I

CATHERINE PARR

OR

ALEXANDER'S HORSE

SCENE.—*London.. Breakfast chamber in the Palace.
KING HENRY VIII and CATHERINE PARR are
discovered sitting opposite to each other at the
breakfast table. The KING has just cracked a
boiled egg.*

KING HENRY. My egg's raw. It really is too
bad.

CATHERINE. Yesterday you complained of their
being hard.

KING HENRY. And so they were. I don't want
a hard egg, and I don't want a raw egg. I want them
to be cooked just right.

CATHERINE. You are very difficult to please. The
egg was in boiling water for three minutes and a half.
I boiled it myself. But give it me. I like them like
that. I will boil you another.

KING HENRY. No, it's too late now. But it is a
fact that you have no idea how to boil an egg. I
wish you'd let them do them in the kitchen.

CATHERINE. If they're done in the kitchen you

complain because they're not here when you come down, and if they are here, you say they're cold.

KING HENRY. I never say anything of the kind. The cook boils eggs beautifully.

CATHERINE. She shall boil them to-morrow.

KING HENRY. One would have thought that a woman of your experience might at least know how to boil an egg. I hate a watery egg. (*Pensively*) Poor dear Katie used to boil eggs beautifully.

CATHERINE. Do you mean Catherine Howard or Katharine of Aragon?

KING HENRY. I was alluding to poor, dear, misguided Katie Howard. Katharine of Aragon never was my wife. The marriage was not valid.

CATHERINE. Well, Catherine Howard ought to have known how to boil eggs, considering her mother was a kitchenmaid.

KING HENRY. That is utterly untrue. Her mother was a Rochford.

CATHERINE. You're thinking of Anne Bullen.

KING HENRY. Yes, yes, to be sure, Katie's mother was a Somerset.

CATHERINE. You're thinking of Jane Seymour.

KING HENRY. Not at all. Jane Seymour was a sister of Somerset's.

CATHERINE. All I know is that Catherine Howard's mother was a kitchenmaid. And I think it's very unkind of you to mention her to me. I suppose you mean that you wish she were alive, and that you loved her better than you love me.

KING HENRY. I never said anything of the kind. All I said was that she knew how to boil eggs.

CATHERINE. You clearly meant to say that she had all the qualities which I lack.

KING HENRY. You are most unfair. I never meant to hint at any such thing. All I said was that I hate a watery egg, and my egg this morning was raw.

CATHERINE (*rising and going to the door in a temper*). Well, the best thing you can do is to get rid of me, and to marry some one who knows how to boil an egg.

KING HENRY. Catherine, come back! I really didn't mean to offend you. You know how to boil eggs very well.

CATHERINE (*sitting down*). One takes an endless amount of trouble, and that's all the thanks one gets. Don't think that I shall ever boil your eggs for you again, because I shan't.

KING HENRY. I was thinking we might have a little music this morning. I have composed a new ballad which I should like to try over with you. It's for viol and lute and voice. We might try it.

CATHERINE. I'm not sure if I have time. What is it called?

KING HENRY. It's called " The Triumph of Love," and it begins :

> Come list to Alexander's deed,
> Great Jove's immortal son,
> Who, riding on a snow-white steed,
> To Babylon did come.

CATHERINE. " Son " doesn't rhyme with " come."
KING HENRY. It's not meant to. It's assonance.
CATHERINE. Do you mean Alexander the Great?
KING HENRY. Yes, of course.
CATHERINE. The only thing is, his horse was black.

KING HENRY. No, my dear, you're mistaken; his horse was white.

CATHERINE. Black—black as jet.

KING HENRY. But I know for a fact it was white.

CATHERINE. Alexander's horse was black. Everybody knows it was black.

KING HENRY. It was white. You can ask any one you like.

CATHERINE. It was black. He was famous for his black horse. There are hundreds of pictures of him on his *black* horse—my father has got one.

KING HENRY. Then the painter made a mistake. Plutarch, Xenophon, Aristotle all mention his *white* horse.

CATHERINE. Black.

KING HENRY. But, my dear, how obstinate you are ! I *know* it is white——

CATHERINE. Black, *coal*-black.

KING HENRY. Have you read Xenophon?

CATHERINE. You are thinking of something else. Even when we were children my father always showed us the picture of Alexander's *black* horse.

KING HENRY. Well, I can easily prove it to you. There's a Plutarch here in the bookcase. (*He goes to the bookcase and takes out a book.*)

CATHERINE I remember it particularly well because my brother had a black horse and we called it " Bucephalus," after Alexander's *black* horse.

KING HENRY (*turning over the leaves of the book*). If it had been black it would never have been called Bucephalus—it would be absurd to call a black horse Bucephalus.

CATHERINE. Not so absurd as calling a white horse Bucephalus.

KING HENRY. He would never have chosen a black horse. He was superstitious——

CATHERINE. Just because you're superstitious and believe in Saints, and worship images, you think every one else is. As a matter of fact, he chose a black horse on purpose to show he didn't care a pin about superstitions——

KING HENRY. Here it is—" χαλεπὸς εἶναι καὶ κομιδῇ δύσχρηστος "—" The horse was wild and extremely difficult to manage." In fact, he had all the characteristics of the white Thessalian horses of that day.

CATHERINE. But it doesn't say it was white. And Thessalian horses are famous for being black.

KING HENRY. You really are too obstinate for words. I will find you the proofs in Xenophon. It is distinctly stated that the horse is *white*. It is an historical fact. Nobody has ever disputed it.

CATHERINE. But Plutarch, you see, practically says it was black.

KING HENRY. Plutarch says nothing of the kind. Besides, I now remember talking about this with Wolsey, who was an excellent scholar. I distinctly remember his saying one day : " As white as Bucephalus." It's quite a common phrase among scholars.

CATHERINE. He must have said " As black as Bucephalus."

KING HENRY. Of course, if you mean to say I tell lies——

CATHERINE. I don't mean that you tell lies, but you are mistaken—that's all.

KING HENRY. But I tell you that there is no mistake possible. I know it as well as I know my own name.

CATHERINE. Your memory plays you tricks. Jus¹ now you couldn't remember Catherine Howard's mother's name.

KING HENRY. That's nothing to do with it. Besides, I did remember it. I made a slip, that's all. But this is an historical fact which I've known all my life.

CATHERINE. I quite understand your memory failing you. You have so many names to remember. I expect you were confusing Alexander's black horse with King Alfred's white horse—the white horse of Wantage.

KING HENRY. Good gracious! If you had a smattering of education you wouldn't say such things! It comes of having no religion and no education, and of not knowing Latin. A Lutheran education is worse than none. Even Anne of Cleves knew Latin.

CATHERINE. Thank Heavens, I don't know Latin! Stupid, superstitious language, fit only for bigots and monks!

KING HENRY. I suppose you mean I am a bigot.

CATHERINE. You can turn what one says into meaning anything you like. As a matter of fact, all I said was that the horse was black.

KING HENRY. I'd rather be a bigot than a Lutheran heretic.

CATHERINE. You know you're wrong and you try to escape the point. That's just like a Tudor. No Tudor could ever listen to reason.

KING HENRY. I must ask you not to insult my family.

CATHERINE. You've insulted mine, which is a

far older one.   My family has no blood on its escutcheon.

KING HENRY.   I won't stand this any longer.   (*He gets up, opens the door, and calls*) Denny, Butts, Page, who is there?

Enter a PAGE

PAGE.   Your Majesty.

KING HENRY.   Go and tell the Lord Chamberlain to make the necessary arrangements for transporting the Ex-Queen to the Tower.

PAGE (*puzzled*).   Yes, your Majesty.   Does your Majesty mean the late Queen's remains? "

KING HENRY.   I said the *Ex*-Queen, you stupid boy—Queen Catherine Parr.

PAGE.   Yes, your Majesty.

KING HENRY.   And tell him to give orders to the Governor of the Tower to have everything ready for the Ex-Queen's execution.

PAGE.   Is the same ceremonial to be observed as in the case of Queen Catherine Howard, your Majesty?

KING HENRY.   Yes; only there need only be one roll of drums instead of two—at the end.   (*The* PAGE *goes to the door*.)   And on the way ask Dr. Butts whether Alexander the Great's horse was black or white.

CATHERINE.   It was black.   (*The* PAGE *bows and goes out*.)   Well, since I'm to be executed, I daresay you will allow me to go and pack up my things.   By the way, you left your lute in my sitting-room yesterday.   I will bring it down.

KING HENRY.   Wait a minute, there's no hurry.

CATHERINE. I beg your pardon, I have very little time, and a great many letters to write.

KING HENRY (*hesitating*). And I wanted to have some music.

CATHERINE. You don't expect me to accompany you now, I suppose? You had better find some one else. I have got other things to think about during my last moments on earth.

KING HENRY (*laughing uneasily*). I was only joking, of course, my dear. You don't mean to say you took it seriously.

CATHERINE. I am afraid I don't appreciate that kind of joke.

KING HENRY. Come, come; let bygones be bygones, and let us have some music. I want to play you my ballad.

Enter the PAGE

PAGE. If you please, your Majesty, I can't find the Lord Chamberlain, and Dr. Butts says your Majesty was quite correct as to the colour of Alexander the Great's horse.

KING HENRY (*beaming*). Very good; you can go. You need not deliver the message to the Lord Chamberlain. (*The* PAGE *bows and retires.*) And now, my dear, we'll go and play. You see, I knew I was right.

[*The* KING *opens the door with a bow.*

CATHERINE. It was black, all the same.

KING HENRY (*indulgently, as if speaking to a child*). Yes, yes, my dear, of course it was black, but let's go and have some music.

[*They go out*

CURTAIN.

II

THE DRAWBACK

SCENE.—*A Corner in Kensington Gardens. A summer evening. Discovered, sitting on a seat, a girl, aged 21, pretty and neat, and a good-looking young man, aged 27, dressed in a top hat and a black morning coat.*

HE. But are you quite sure you will not change your mind?

SHE. I never change my mind once it is made up. I often take a very long time to make up my mind, but once I've made it up I never change. Now my sister Alice is quite different. She never knows her mind from one minute to the other.

HE. But your father——

SHE. Papa always does what I want. Besides, directly he knows you it will be all right. And when he knows that you're at the Bar he will be delighted. He always wanted me to marry a lawyer. You see Papa was at the Bar in his young days—I daresay your father was too.

HE (*embarrassed*). No, yes—I mean no. That's to say he is in a way indirectly connected with the Bar; but my father's principal hobby is playing on the harp. He gives himself up almost entirely to that now.

SHE.　I see.

HE.　Have you told your father yet?

SHE.　You told me I wasn't to until I'd seen you again.

HE.　Yes, of course. I thought you might have changed your mind.

SHE.　As if that were likely.

HE.　And then, if you remember, I told you when I, when you, when we settled everything that there was a—er—drawback.

SHE.　As if any drawback could possibly make any difference.

HE.　I thought it might.

SHE.　You mean to say that it is something which might make me wish to change my mind?

HE.　Exactly.

SHE.　That shows you know me very little—but what is it?

HE.　You see it's a kind of confession.

SHE.　I know what it is; you want to tell me you once loved some one else.

HE.　No, not that, I swear I never did. I may have thought once or twice that I was in love, but until I met you I never knew what love, what real love, was.

SHE.　And those other times when you thought you were in love—were there many of them?

HE.　It only happened twice; that's to say three times, only the third time didn't count.

SHE.　And the first time, who was she?

HE.　I was quite young, only a boy. She was a girl in an A.B.C. shop.

SHE.　Was she pretty?

HE.　Not exactly.

SHE. Did you propose to her?

HE. Yes, but she refused.

SHE. And that's all that happened?

HE. That's all.

SHE. And the second time?

HE. It was the parson's daughter down in the country.

SHE. Did you make love to her?

HE. No, not really, of course, but we were friends.

SHE. Did you kiss her?

HE. Only once, and that was by accident. But it was all years ago.

SHE. How many years ago?

HE. Let me see; two, no, no, it must have been four years ago. I'm not sure it wasn't five. She married the curate.

SHE. And the third time?

HE. Oh! that was nothing.

SHE. Who was she?

HE. She was an artist—a singer.

SHE. A concert singer?

HE. Almost; that's to say she wanted to be one. She sang in a music-hall.

SHE. Oh!

HE. Only a *serious* turn. She wasn't dressed up or anything. She sang " The Lost Chord " and songs like that. She was called " The New Zealand Nightingale."

SHE. And you knew her?

HE. Very slightly. I had tea with her once or twice. And then she went away.

SHE. Back to New Zealand?

HE. Yes, back to New Zealand.

SHE. **Now** I've made you confess everything.

Aren't you glad you've got it off your mind? I don't mind a bit, and I like you for being so honest.

HE.   But it's not that at all. It's nothing to do with me.

SHE.   Then who has it got to do with?

HE.   My father.

SHE.   You mean he wont approve of me?

HE.   Of course I don't mean that. He'd simply love you.

SHE.   He's going to marry again.

HE.   No, it's not that.

SHE.   He doesn't want you to marry.

HE.   No, it's nothing to do with me.

SHE.   Then I don't understand.

HE.   It's something to do with him.

SHE.   He's consumptive.

HE.   No; his health is excellent.

SHE.   He's lost his money.

HE.   No; he's very well off. You see it's something to do with his social position. A matter of— I don't quite know how to put it.

SHE.   But, Georgie, you don't think I'm such a snob as to care twopence for social position and conventions of that kind? Your father is your father— that's all that matters, isn't it?

HE.   I know, I know, but there are prejudices.

SHE.   Is it something your father's done? Has he been in the Bankruptcy Court? I wouldn't care a pin.

HE.   No, it's nothing he's done. It's something he *is*.

SHE.   He's a Socialist !

HE.   No.

SHE.   Is he a Roman Catholic?

HE. Oh, no ! He's Church of England.

SHE. I know; he's a Liberal.

HE. No; he says the Liberals are just as bad as the Conservatives.

SHE. Then he's a little Englander.

HE. On the contrary; he's outside politics. He belongs to no party.

SHE. He's a foreigner—by birth, I mean.

HE. Not at all.

SHE. He's not a Mormon?

HE. No. It's nothing to do with politics or religion or that kind of thing. It's his profession.

SHE. His profession ! But I thought—as if I cared about his profession !

HE. But you might—there are some professions——

SHE. You see, I know he's honest.

HE. Oh ! you needn't have any fear. He's perfectly honest, respectable, and respected.

SHE. Then what is it ?

HE. I'd rather you guessed it.

SHE. How absurd you are ! I know what it is; he's somebody's agent.

HE. No.

SHE. Then he's a schoolmaster.

HE. No.

SHE (*tentatively*). Of course, I know he was never in trade?

HE. No, never. He has had nothing to do with it

SHE. Is he on the stage?

HE. No; he disapproves of actors.

SHE. He's a Quaker.

HE. I told you it's nothing to do with religion.

SHE. Then, he's a photographer. Some photographers almost count as artists.

HE.   No.

SHE.   Then it is something to do with art.

HE.   His profession certainly needs art and skill.

SHE.   He's not a conjurer?

HE.   Conjurers are scarcely respectable.

SHE.   I know, of course.   He's a jockey.

HE.   No.

SHE.   A bookmaker.

HE.   No.

SHE.   A veterinary surgeon.

HE.   No.

SHE.   Does he ever give lessons?

HE.   Only to his assistants, whom he's training.

SHE.   He's a prize-fighter.

HE.   Oh, no !

SHE.   He's an Art-dressmaker.

HE.   No.   You see it's something some people might mind.

SHE.   What can it be.   A dentist.

HE.   No.

SHE.   How stupid of me.   He's a literary man.

HE.   He's never written a line.

SHE.   But you told me.   I remember now.   He plays the harp.   He's something musical; but nobody could mind that.   He's a dancing-master.

HE.   No.

SHE.   A commercial traveller.

HE.   No.

SHE.   Of course not; it's something to do with art.   But what could one mind?

HE.   Not exactly art.   It's more skill.

SHE.   Is he a chiropodist?

HE.   No.

SHE. Or a Swedish masseur?

HE. Nothing like it.

SHE. Is it anything to do with officials?

HE. Yes, in a way.

SHE. Then I've guessed it. He's a detective.

HE. No.

SHE. He's in the Secret Service.

HE. No.

SHE. It's something to do with the police.

HE. Not exactly.

SHE. With prisons.

HE. In a way.

SHE. He's a prison inspector.

HE. No.

SHE. A prison chaplain.

HE. No; he's not in Orders.

SHE. The prison doctor who has to feed the Suffragettes.

HE. No.

SHE. I've guessed. He's a keeper in a lunatic asylum.

HE. You're getting cold again.

SHE. Then it's something to do with prisons?

HE. Yes.

SHE. He's a warder.

HE. No.

SHE. I don't know who else is in a prison, except the prisoners.

HE. He doesn't live in the prison.

SHE. But he goes there sometimes?

HE. Yes.

SHE. I give it up.

HE. His duty is a disagreeable one, but some one has to do it.

SHE. He's the man who has to taste the prisoners' food.

HE. I didn't know there was such a person.

SHE. You must tell me. I'll never guess.

HE (*blurting it out*). Well, you see, he's the hang-man.

[*A Pause.*

SHE. You mean he——

HE. Yes, he——

SHE. Oh, I see.

HE. Some people might mind this. He's going to retire very soon—on a pension.

SHE. Yes?

HE. And, of course, he very seldom——

SHE. Yes, I suppose——

HE. It's all quite private, of course.

SHE. Yes, of course.   [*A Pause.*

(*Looking at her watch*) Good gracious! I shall be late for dinner. It's nearly seven o'clock. I must fly. I was late yesterday.

HE. Shall I—shall we meet to-morrow?

SHE. No, not to-morrow. I'm busy all to-morrow.

HE. Perhaps the day after.

SHE. Perhaps I had better tell you at once what I was going to write to you.

HE. You think the drawback——

SHE (*indignantly*). I wasn't thinking of that. But I do think you ought to have told me directly about those others.

HE. What others?

SHE. Those women—the A.B.C. shop, the clergy-man's daughter, and that music hall singer.

HE. But you said you didn't mind.

SHE. I minded too much to speak about it. A

music-hall singer! The New Zealand Nightingale! Oh! to think that you, that I——Oh! the shame of it.

HE. But——

SHE. There's no but. You've grossly deceived me. You played with my feelings. You led me on. You trifled with me. You've treated me scandalously. You've broken my heart. You've ruined my life.

HE. But let me say one word.

SHE. Not one word. A girl in an A.B.C. shop! A clergyman's daughter! and a music-hall singer!

HE. You really mean——

SHE. I've heard quite enough. Thank you, Mr. Belleville. Please to understand that our acquaintance is at an end. Good evening. (*She bows and walks away.*)

CURTAIN.

III

PIOUS ÆNEAS

SCENE.—*A room in* DIDO'S *Palace at Carthage. Discovered :* ÆNEAS, *wearing a cloak of Tyrian purple ;* SERESTUS *and* SERGESTUS.

ÆNEAS (*in a sharp military tone*). Is everything ready?

SERESTUS. Aye, aye, sir.

ÆNEAS. No leave for either watch to-night. We shall probably go to sea to-morrow morning at four. I'll let you know later.

SERESTUS. Aye, aye, sir.

ÆNEAS. That's all. Don't any of you get talking, and you, Sergestus, report seven minutes to noon to me.

SERGESTUS. Aye, aye, sir.

[SERGESTUS *and* SERESTUS *salute and go out L.*

[ÆNEAS *unrolls a chart.*

DIDO *enters through a curtain C.* ÆNEAS *hastily conceals the chart.*

DIDO (*cheerfully*). Well?

ÆNEAS. Good morning.

DIDO. Are you busy? If so I won't disturb you.

ÆNEAS. No, no, I'm not at all busy.

DIDO. I thought you were reading something when I came in.

ÆNEAS. I was only looking through some accounts.

DIDO. Aren't you cold in this room? Wouldn't you like a fire?

ÆNEAS. No, thank you. I don't feel the cold.

DIDO. It's blowing so hard to-day. I've been for a walk.

ÆNEAS. Oh, is it? I haven't been out this morning.

DIDO. I went for quite a long walk, past the quays.

ÆNEAS. Do you think that was wise? You ought to be careful in this cold weather.

DIDO. I like the cold. It reminds me of the day you came. Do you remember how cold you all were?

ÆNEAS. Yes.

DIDO. I'm sure you're busy. I'm sure I'm disturbing you.

ÆNEAS. Not in the least, I promise you.

DIDO. Æneas.

ÆNEAS. Well?

DIDO. I've guessed!

ÆNEAS (*uneasy and alarmed*). What? I don't understand.

DIDO (*smiling*). Your little surprise.

ÆNEAS. What surprise?

DIDO. I meant not to say, but I can't help it. I found it out this morning by accident. I think it's too dear of you to take all this trouble for me, and to send a *whole* fleet to Tyre to bring me back that purple dye which you promised me—the same colour as your cloak, which *I* gave you. I meant to pretend I didn't know, but I am so touched I can't help it.

ÆNEAS. Oh! the expedition to Tyre. Yes, I was thinking——

DIDO. And when do they start?

ÆNEAS. It isn't quite settled. It depends.

DIDO. Couldn't we go a part of the way with them?

ÆNEAS. No, I'm afraid that's quite out of the question. The time of year, you see, is so bad. I don't think you would enjoy it at all. It's very cold and the sea will be rough.

DIDO. I love a rough sea. Couldn't we go as far as Sicily with them? They're going to stop there.

ÆNEAS. I don't think you could leave Carthage just at this moment, could you?

DIDO. No, that's true. We couldn't very well leave Carthage just now, could we? Because King Iarbas has sent another threatening message.

ÆNEAS. Again?

DIDO. Yes; he threatens to attack Carthage at once. He cannot get over the fact that we really are married, and that I have a brave, dear, faithful, darling husband to love and protect me for ever and ever.

ÆNEAS. It certainly is most awkward.

DIDO. What? What does it matter to us what he says and does?

ÆNEAS. Well, the fact is that I shall probably have to go with the fleet.

DIDO. Then I'll come with you.

ÆNEAS. My dear Elissa, that's impossible.

DIDO. You don't mean to say that you're going to leave me—your wife—alone and unprotected, to face the invasion of a powerful, savage, and angry king when there is absolutely no necessity for your going at all?

ÆNEAS. I can't possibly leave the fleet to Palinurus—our only pilot. Quite between ourselves he doesn't know how to navigate—he once mistook the Charybdis beacon for a star . . . it was after supper. . . .

DIDO. Dearest, I quite understand. You must put off the expedition. I promise you not to mind. I don't really want the purple dye. We'll wait till the season is more propitious. It was most dear of you to think of it.

ÆNEAS. But I'm afraid it can't be put off.

DIDO. Why?

ÆNEAS. Well, you see I have absolutely promised—I have definitely pledged myself—I have given my word of honour to visit my brother Eryx in Sicily.

DIDO. You can put that off until the spring.

ÆNEAS. I'm afraid it would be too late then. You see the whole matter is most complicated. Eryx expects me. I promised him to go, and if I don't go now——

DIDO. What will happen?

ÆNEAS (*vaguely*). He won't be there.

DIDO. Why? Is he going away?

ÆNEAS. And then there's another matter which is still more important. I simply must visit my father's tomb in Sicily.

DIDO. You might have thought of that before.

ÆNEAS. I have constantly—but I put it off.

DIDO. As you have put it off so long already, you may just as well put it off a little longer.

ÆNEAS. Yes, but there's Jove.

DIDO. What has Jove got to do with it?

ÆNEAS. He wishes me to go. He is anxious that I should go to Sicily and (*pauses*) to Italy.

DIDO. Why to Italy?

ÆNEAS. It's entirely for my boy's sake, Ascanius . . . to establish a home for him.

DIDO. And how long will you stay there?

ÆNEAS. It depends how things turn out.

DIDO. A month?

ÆNEAS. I'm afraid it will be a little longer than that.

DIDO. Six weeks?

ÆNEAS. You see it all depends on Jove.

DIDO. I ask you as a favour to put off the whole thing until the spring.

ÆNEAS. You know I would do anything you ask me, but I'm afraid I can't do that. I would if I could, but I can't.

DIDO. You mean you are determined to go to Italy.

ÆNEAS. It's the last thing I wish to do personally, but Jove——

DIDO. Please leave Jove out of the discussion.

ÆNEAS. After all I must go there some time or other.

DIDO. You are tired of me.

ÆNEAS. How can you say such a thing?

DIDO. I knew it at once. You are going to Italy, and you're never coming back.

ÆNEAS. Of course I shall come back some time.

DIDO (*violently*). Then it's true! I knew you were tired of me! I've known it for a long time; but I never thought you could be so despicably mean as to try to go away without saying a word.

ÆNEAS. But I never dreamt——

DIDO. You build a fleet on the sly, in the middle of winter, to go to a strange country where you have no ties.

ÆNEAS. I beg your pardon, there's my brother——

DIDO. When wind and weather are at their worst, simply and solely to get away from me——

ÆNEAS. But I swear——

DIDO. Oh! you don't expect me to believe for a moment all that nonsense about Jove. If you wanted to stay you wouldn't think twice about Jove. You don't care a pin what may happen to me. You have set everybody against me; even my relations, my brother, all the Numidians, and the whole of Libya. You've ruined my reputation and given me over to my enemies, and then you put it all upon Jove.

ÆNEAS. I beg you to listen, Elissa. I had never for a moment meant to conceal my journey.

DIDO. Then why tell all those silly lies about Tyre and the purple dye?

ÆNEAS. I never said a word about Tyre and the purple dye. It was you.

DIDO. How can you tell such lies? When I asked you if the fleet was going to Tyre you distinctly said Yes.

ÆNEAS. What I did say was that I was obliged to go to Sicily to visit my father's tomb. That is the simple truth. You can't expect me to wish the whole world to think me unfilial! As it is, I haven't had a night's rest for months. My father's ghost appears to me every night.

DIDO. You expect me——

ÆNEAS. Please let me finish. And only yesterday I received a direct command from Jove, saying I was to go to Italy at once and found a kingdom there. Of course, if this only concerned myself I shouldn't care, but there's my son Ascanius to be thought of. I have no right to defraud him of his kingdom. If it were a question of inclination of course I should stay here, and Italy's the last place I want to go to. If I went anywhere I should go to Troy; but Jove has made my duty plain, and after all a man must do his duty.

DIDO. Your duty! And I suppose it was a part of your duty to deceive me, to ruin me, to stir up enemies against me, and then to leave me defenceless! Me, your wife!

ÆNEAS (*angrily*). I must point out that I warned you at the time that our marriage was in no sense legal or valid—it could never be recognised as an alliance.

DIDO (*calmly*). You are quite right. It is entirely my fault. I thought you were a man of honour. I believed your word. I thought you were a man. I was mistaken. You are only a Trojan. I found you shipwrecked, an outcast, starving, helpless, at death's door. I saved your fleet. I rescued your comrades from death. I saved you from destruction. And this is my reward. The Greeks were right when they burned Troy to the ground, killed your men and made your women into slaves. They were right to spare you, because you are not a man. Your place is with the menials. Please don't think I shall prevent you going to Italy. Don't imagine for a moment I am going to argue with you. By all means go and found a kingdom. I trust you will enjoy it and that it will turn out better than Troy. I am sure you know best, and I am sure you know what is best, and I am sure you are right. Don't imagine that I mind, or that I shall miss you, for I shan't. I am not in the least annoyed at your going, I am only surprised and vexed to find that a man who I thought was honourable, and truthful, and brave should turn out to be dishonourable, a liar, a coward —and a mean coward. I am angry with myself for having made such a mistake about a man, and that you, by your foolish, silly, transparent lies and shuffling should have shown me what a poor opinion you have of me. I wish you a very pleasant journey, and I hope you will do your duty in Italy as well as you have done it in Carthage.

[*She goes out C.*

ÆNEAS (*wiping his forehead with a handkerchief*). That's over !

Enter SERGESTUS *R.*

SERGESTUS. Seven minutes to noon, sir.

ÆNEAS. It's all right. We go to sea to-morrow.

SERGESTUS. Aye, aye, sir.

[ÆNEAS *goes out, whistling the tune " Good-bye, Carthage, I must leave you."*

CURTAIN.

IV

THE DEATH OF ALEXANDER

SCENE FROM A TRAGEDY.—"*The Life and Death of Alexander.*" Anon. [Old Plays. Printed for *Peter Buck*, at the sign of the *Temple*, near the *Inner-Temple-gate* in *Fleet-street*, 1701.]

ACT **V.** SCENE IV.—*Babylon. A bed-chamber in* ALEXANDER'S *Palace.* ALEXANDER *sleeping in bed ;* ROXANA *attending.*

ROXANA. Full thrice hath Phœbus bath'd in
    Neptune's flood,
Thrice hath the pale-fac'd moon increas'd and wan'd,
But Alexander is uncomforted.
Not watchful care, nor drugs, nor natural simples
Can hold at bay the sickness which pursues him.
Methinks that treason whets his murderous knife,
And meditates a foul and bloody deed.
I dare not sleep. Have pity on my woes,
Immortal gods ! I know not friends from foes !

Enter a SLAVE

SLAVE. Madam.
ROXANA. I know thou bringest some ill news.
SLAVE. Good madam, there is treason in the
    palace.
The Queen Statira, envious of thy issue,

Is plotting murder.   She hath a strange syrup,
Brew'd by a wizard in Arabia,
More direful than the hebenon which Medea
Did cull in Colchos by the yawning graves.
She purposes, when sleep shall seize thee wholly,
To give my Lord o' the juice.

    ROXANA.   I thank you, slave,
I thank you, here is gold.

    SLAVE.   I thank you, madam.

            [*Exit* SLAVE.   ROXANA *feigns sleep*.

Enter QUEEN STATIRA

    STATIRA.   My Lord, I come to say a last fare-
    well.
Perchance the lying mist which seal'd thine eyes
Shall dissipate and we may be aton'd;
And, deaf to false Roxana, thou'lt prefer
Thy Royal spouse, and cancel and defy
Her bastard's claim.

    ROXANA.   Hence! hence, foul murd'ress hence!
Thou cursed thief who in the midnight season
Dost come to filch Great Alexander's soul
With mixture dire of hellish property,
Begone!   Thy treason is made palpable,
Thy baleful juice is harmless as pure water,
And thy dread weapon, turning on thyself,
Shall compass thine own ignomy.

    STATIRA.   Vain fool!
Thy scolding frights me not.   I am Statira.
Nor canst thou with false accusation
Raze from this brow the seal of royalty,
Nor take away the sov'ranty of birth.
Albeit supplanted by a saucy caitiff,

Albeit slighted, I was once a Queen;
And I am still the daughter of Darius,
The King, whom kneeling Emperors called the
    Great.
Farewell, my Lord, with no more dreadful purpose
Have I come hither, than to say farewell.
I was thy spouse, and I will not importune
A faithless husband with a faithfulness
Unprofitable. So my Lord, farewell.

        [*Exit* STATIRA. ALEXANDER *wakes*.

ALEXANDER. Roxana, take thy lute. My soul is
    heavy.
Sing me asleep with music, let me rest.

SONG

    'Twas in the merry month of May,
      When the sweet birds do sing,
    That Proserpine—ah! lack-a-day!—
      Did go a-gathering.
    She stoop'd and cull'd the violet,
    The pansy and the oxlip wet.

    But gloomy Dis the maid espied,
      And yoked his horses six,
    And in his wagon drove a bride
      Across the doleful Styx.
    'Twas in the merry month of May
    She gathered flowers. Ah! lack-a-day!

ALEXANDER. I thank you, 'tis a lulling melody
I am a-weary. Sleep, impiteous sleep,
Unmitigable, uncorruptible gaoler,
Come, cloak my senses with thy leaden robe,
Lead me to durance in thy drowsy cell.

Enter DOCTOR

DOCTOR.   How doth my Lord?

ROXANA.   Ill, ill beyond the power
Of simples, drugs, and physician's art.
In slumb'ry perturbation he'll converse
With images of his distemper'd fancy;
Or he will bid me touch the instrument
And soothe his fever'd spirit with a strain.

DOCTOR.   Are you not weary?   It is now three
    nights
That you have watch'd.

ROXANA.   The canker of sharp grief,
The sleepless sorrow gnawing at my heart
Doth countervail outwearied nature's claim.
I shall not sleep till Alexander wakes
To health, or till he sleeps to wake no more.
But, softly.   See, he stirs.

DOCTOR.   Good night, sweet lady.

ROXANA.   Good night to you.

                    [*Exit* DOCTOR.   ROXANA *sleeps*.

ALEXANDER.   The galleys ride at anchor !
To-morrow we'll set sail for Italy,
Nor rest until we've pitch'd our tent in Rome,
And snatch'd the insolent jewel of the West.
But yesterday the Afric oracle
Bespake to me an unconfined sway,
An orb and empery unparallel'd.
And thence, when the barbarians of the West
Are mild as leashed hounds beneath our yoke,
And when each sev'ral province hath subscrib'd,
To India we'll retrace our eager steps
And reach the undiscover'd sea beyond.
By the lush banks of Ganges, Alexander

Shall build a temple to his royal sire,
Great Jupiter.   Thence we'll to Babylon,
And plant there our abiding seat of rule—
In the fix'd centre of the universe.
North, south, and east and west shall our dominion,
Like the spread rays of gold Hyperion,
Pierce to the distant corners of the globe.
Oh look, Seleucus, look, Hephæstion,
Look, the swarth King in jewell'd burgonet,
All clinquant, mounted on an elephant,
Advances with his congregated host.
On, veterans !   On, on, Bucephalus !
The ford !   The ford !   The villains fly ! Come,
    Ho !
Clitus, awake, Roxana, O.

   ROXANA.   My Lord?
   ALEXANDER.   Didst thou cry out?
   ROXANA.   My Lord, I was asleep,
And knew not that I cried.
   ALEXANDER.   Give me to drink.
Methought I was once more in India,
Crying my veterans to victory
Across the enchafed surges of Hydaspes.
My spirit fails.   Come near to me, Roxana,
That I may breathe my last in fond adieu.
   ROXANA.   Drink, my Lord, of this potion. It is
    mix'd
   Of herb-grace by a sure apothecary.
   ALEXANDER.   Farewell, Roxana. Hie thee to my
    mother,
Olympias, and tell her that I die
Her name upon my lips, a dutiful son.
Salute her with deep duty, say I needed
Her tenderness ; say that I am the shadow,

The mockery and ruins of her boy
Who manag'd and bestrid Bucephalus.
Remain with her, and let our only child
Be nurs'd and school'd in martial exercise,
And taught, as I was taught, philosophy.
Farewell, adieu ! The last of all the Greeks
Hath gone to meet Achilles.

ROXANA. O my Lord !

Enter MESSENGER

MESSENGER. Most gracious liege, the veterans are here,
They press without.

ALEXANDER. They shall be welcome. Ho !
Come quickly, veterans, or I am dead.

ROXANA. My Lord ! My husband !

Enter VETERANS

ALEXANDER. Friends, farewell to you,
Friends all and brothers all and countrymen,
Born of one soil in Macedonia,
Tell Macedon of how we fought together
Beyond Hydaspes. Grieve not overmuch,
That with the world half-conquer'd I must die,
Not fighting, but in bed, and like a woman.
I, to whom earth's huge globe was all too small,
Must occupy a niggard urn of dust.
I am for India. Come, Bucephalus,
One charge and we are masters of the world !

[*Dies*.

ROXANA. Great Alexander's dead. That soaring spirit
Which fretted in the confines of the world,

Hath broken from its circumscribing clay.
Hyperion himself was not so bright,
Nor Mars so bold.   Our Orient sun hath set.
Ashy eclipse shall darken the stale world :
Asia and Egypt to the furthest Ind,
And Greece, and Macedon, where he was born,
Shall mingle tears of everlasting woe.
Come bear his body hence, and build a pyre
More lofty than the walls of Babylon ;
And when the funeral's done, we'll bear his urn,
Obsequiously in sad procession,
Across the Libyan desert, to the grove
Where stands the Temple of his father Jove.

CURTAIN.

V

THE GREEK VASE

SCENE.—*A garret on the top floor of a squalid house in the Trastevere, Rome. Discovered:* GIO-VANNI, *a young sculptor, lying in bed, pale and emaciated; he coughs incessantly. The room is quite bare. There are only two chairs and one cupboard. It is very cold. There is no fire. By the bedside sits a prosperous dealer. He wears a frock-coat and a gold pince-nez.*

GIOVANNI (*wearily*). But I tell you it's not for sale.

THE DEALER. You might let me look at it.

GIOVANNI. What is the use? I tell you I won't sell it.

THE DEALER. There can be no harm in your showing it to me.

GIOVANNI (*coughing*). Not to-day. Can't you see that I'm very ill and that talking tires me?

THE DEALER. Very well. I will call again to-morrow.

GIOVANNI. You won't find me at home.

THE DEALER. Are you going away?

GIOVANNI. Yes, on a long journey.

THE DEALER. Abroad?

GIOVANNI. Abroad.

33

THE DEALER. To what country?

GIOVANNI. They have prescribed me change of air. They say it is the only thing which can cure me.

THE DEALER. You are going to the seaside?

GIOVANNI. On the contrary. I am going to be near a river.

THE DEALER. The Arno? Pisa, I suppose?

GIOVANNI. No.

THE DEALER. Not Paris; that would be bad for you.

GIOVANNI. Why do you think Paris would be bad for me?

THE DEALER. In the first place it's very cold there now, and then I don't think a large town is what you need.

GIOVANNI. You are anxious that I should not go to Paris.

THE DEALER. I? Not at all. Why? I merely meant that I thought you needed country air.

GIOVANNI. Yes, a villa on the Riviera for the winter, and another for the summer at Amalfi with a garden of roses; or a chalet in the Tyrol; or perhaps an island in the Tropics with palm trees and a yacht to sail about in—all that would do me good, wouldn't it? One doesn't have to pay for little luxuries like that, does one? They drop from heaven into the pockets of starving artists.

THE DEALER. Now, if you would only be reasonable and show me that vase. I am sure we could make enough money for you to take a trip to Albano. The air there is beautiful.

GIOVANNI. Very well, you may see it. It's in the cupboard

[*The* DEALER *goes to the cupboard and takes out
a large black circular Greek vase with figures
painted on it. He observes it carefully.*

THE DEALER. This is not, of course, up to your
best form. I won't say that it is valueless. There
is, however, very little market now for this kind of
thing, and if I bought it I should probably have it
on my hands for years.

GIOVANNI. You needn't trouble about that. The
vase is not for sale.

THE DEALER. But in the peculiar circumstances,
and since we have done business together for so many
years, I am willing to make an exception in this case.
How much do you want for it?

GIOVANNI (*savagely*). I tell you it's not for sale.

THE DEALER. Now, be reasonable. I will give
forty lire for it.

GIOVANNI. You amuse me immensely.

THE DEALER. The vase is of no particular use to
me, and the fashion changes so quickly. Collectors
now are mad about Egypt and Japan. Greece is
finished. It's old, finished. Why, collectors now
prefer even Roman things to Greek. Giordani
says——

GIOVANNI. You are wasting your breath.

THE DEALER. I will give you forty-five lire. Mind
you, that's an enormous price, because, I repeat, the
vase is not up to your usual standard.

GIOVANNI. Please put the vase down on this
chair, there, next me. (*The* DEALER *puts the vase
down on the chair next to* GIOVANNI.) Thank you.
Now I wish you would go away. I am tired. You
tire me. (*He coughs.*)

THE DEALER. Now, instead of a vase, if it had only

been a Japanese idol or a Renaissance figure, it would be a very different matter.

GIOVANNI. When you bought my Simonetta you said there was no demand for Renaissance work.

THE DEALER. That was three years ago. It was perfectly true then. The fashion changes so quickly.

GIOVANNI. I won't sell the vase.

THE DEALER. Then, how do you propose to live?

GIOVANNI. Perhaps I have found a patron.

THE DEALER. Ah! Who is he?

GIOVANNI. You would like to know, wouldn't you?

THE DEALER. I wouldn't believe it of you. I know you are far too honest to violate all the canons of business etiquette and to play off one patron against another. You have always dealt with me, and I have always treated you handsomely—most handsomely—you must admit that.

GIOVANNI. How much did you give me for my large terra-cotta bust of Pallas?

THE DEALER. I was mad when I bought that bust. I sold it for a quarter of what I gave you. I had the greatest difficulty in getting rid of it.

GIOVANNI. How much exactly did you give me for it?

THE DEALER. Of course, I could never give you so much as that again.

GIOVANNI (*impatiently*). How much was it?

THE DEALER. I believe it was eighty-five lire. I must have been mad. But times were better then. There is no market for that kind of thing now, none whatever.

GIOVANNI. So much the better for you, then, as you won't lose money over my vase.

THE DEALER. For old acquaintance' sake, I offer you fifty lire; there, you see?

GIOVANNI. You make very good jokes.

THE DEALER. Do you mean to say you think that's too little?

GIOVANNI. I said you make very good jokes. You're a witty fellow.

THE DEALER. You artists are so improvident. You never know how many soldi there are in a lira.

GIOVANNI. You see we don't have very much experience in counting lire. (*He coughs.*)

THE DEALER. Ah! if you only counted the soldi the lire would take care of themselves.

GIOVANNI. We don't always have the chance of counting soldi.

THE DEALER. To think of the position you might be in now if you had only observed the elementary rules of thrift.

GIOVANNI. And to think of the position you are in by my not having done so!

THE DEALER. Yes; here am I obliged, positively forced, to offer you for a trumpery vase at least three times its value, and I give you my word of honour that in offering you fifty-five lire for the vase—for I am going to go as far as that—I shall be out of pocket—out of pocket. Do you understand?

GIOVANNI. I quite understand, only if I were you I shouldn't bring in the word " honour."

THE DEALER. I don't understand.

GIOVANNI. You wouldn't.

THE DEALER. Well, fifty-five lire; it's a bargain!

GIOVANNI. Suppose we talk about something else.

THE DEALER. You are all the same, you

artists. . . . You never will listen to reason. You never will understand that business is business and not——

GIOVANNI. Charity.

THE DEALER. In this case it is charity, pure charity. I would not dream of buying the vase from any one else.

GIOVANNI. I don't expect you would.

THE DEALER. Why, Leonardi sold me only yesterday a little ivory Perseus for thirty lire.

GIOVANNI. I made that Perseus, and you know it; otherwise you wouldn't have bought it.

THE DEALER. Well, I'm a busy man, and I can't waste my time arguing with you. I'll give you sixty lire. That's my last word.

GIOVANNI. It's a great pity you didn't go on the stage.

THE DEALER. You think I'm trying to cheat you. Surely——

GIOVANNI. No, I don't *think* anything of the kind.

THE DEALER. Now, come, let me take the vase. You've got no use for it here. Think what a nice little trip to Albano will do for you.

GIOVANNI (*coughing*). You can't imagine how greatly you tire me.

THE DEALER. I never knew such an obstinate fellow as you are. I'll make it seventy, but this is positively my last word. You can take it or leave it.

GIOVANNI. Oh! Leave it for Heaven's sake. Leave the vase, and leave me. (*He coughs.*)

THE DEALER. You're surely not going to sell it to some one else: you wouldn't be so mean!

GIOVANNI. Who knows?

THE DEALER. That kind of bluff, my friend, won't do with me. I am too old a bird to be caught by a trick. Come now, I offer you seventy lire— seventy whole lire. Do you understand?

GIOVANNI. It's impossible. The vase is disposed of.

THE DEALER. Sold! Impossible! You couldn't do such a thing. You couldn't play me such a shabby trick. Who has bought it?

GIOVANNI. Nobody has bought it.

THE DEALER. You are trifling. It isn't fair. You are wasting my time. You know I'm a busy man.

GIOVANNI. And you are wasting my time, and I am a dying man. They say I can't live twenty-four hours.

THE DEALER. What nonsense! There, you see how foolish you are! Now I tell you what I'll do. I'll give you two hundred lire for the vase. It's unheard of, but in view——

GIOVANNI. I am a dying man, and this is our last bargain. It has consequently no effect on future dealings. The time at your disposal is short; dying men don't bluff, you must have the vase; all this makes your price jump up. Listen to me a moment (*He takes a cutting from a newspaper out of his pocket.*) This is a cutting from an English illustrated newspaper. A friend sent it me. It is the reproduction of a photograph, and under it is written: "The terra-cotta bust of Pallas, a work of the central period of Greek perfection, the age of Pericles, after having been rejected by the British Museum, has been purchased for the Louvre for the sum of £6,000. While congratulating the French nation on their acquisition, we cannot help asking ourselves what the British Museum authorities," etc. I skip. But wait— Here is a further comment which may interest you. " Some of our criticasters have thrown doubts on the authenticity of the vase." Now look at the photograph. Perhaps you recognise the bust.

THE DEALER. You don't mean to say you think——

GIOVANNI (*in a low voice*). Be quiet. You see this vase. (*He takes the vase.*) It's not for sale. It never will be. Do you know why? Because it's my masterpiece, and because it's mine. This is what I'm going to do with it. (*He takes the vase and throws it to the ground, shattering it to fragments.*) and now I can die in peace. Go!

THE DEALER. But——

GIOVANNI. Go! (GIOVANNI *turns his head to the wall.*) [*Exit* DEALER, *mumbling*

CURTAIN.

VI

THE FATAL RUBBER

SCENE.—*A Room in the Palace of the Louvre. Discovered, seated at a card-table:* CHARLES VI. *King of France,* ISABEAU DE BAVIERE, *the Queen, the* DAUPHIN, *and* CATHERINE, *his sister.*

THE KING. I think we might have some clean cards.

THE QUEEN. I won't play with those thick English cards, it takes hours to shuffle them. Besides, I think it's unpatriotic.

THE KING. Rubbish! Games are outside politics.

THE QUEEN. I think it is unpatriotic just now, when the war's gcing on, and I always shall think so.

THE DAUPHIN (*yawning*). What game are we going to play to-night?

THE KING. Pont d'Avignon.

THE QUEEN. Pont d'Avignon.

THE DAUPHIN. Biribi.

CATHERINE. Nain Jaune.

THE QUEEN. We shall, of course, play Pont d'Avignon. Your father wishes it.

THE KING. Cut for partners. (*They cut.*)

THE DAUPHIN. You and I play together, Papa.

[*They change seats so as to be opposite one another.*

THE KING. Cut for deal. (*They cut.*)

THE DAUPHIN. It's Papa's deal. (*The* KING *deals.*)

THE KING. I leave it.

THE DAUPHIN. I make no trumps.

CATHERINE. I double.

THE DAUPHIN. I redouble.

THE QUEEN. We're content.

THE KING. You've no business to say " we're content."

THE QUEEN. We play Hearts, of course, in doubled no trumps.

THE KING. Never; we always play the highest of the shortest. Besides which it's Catherine who doubled.

THE QUEEN. I play Hearts. The Queen of Hearts is called after me, so of course you must play Hearts, Catherine.

THE KING. You ought to have said that before. Besides in this case the rule doesn't apply.

CATHERINE (*playing the two of Hearts to the Dauphin*). Put your cards down, Charles.

[*The* DAUPHIN *puts his hand down. He has got no Hearts ; the ace, King, Knave, ten, and five of Clubs ; ace, Queen, ten, and six of Diamonds ; Queen, Knave, ten, nine of Spades.*

THE KING. That's not a no-trumper. You might have made no trumps if it had been your make. As for redoubling, it's too absurd.

[*The* QUEEN *takes the trick with the Queen of Hearts ; neither the* KING *nor the* DAUPHIN *has got any.*

THE QUEEN. No Hearts. How odd! Then all the rest are ours. I've got nine Hearts now.

THE KING. I beg your pardon. It's not at all so certain.

THE QUEEN. Very well, we'll play it.

CATHERINE. I can see your cards, Papa.

[*They play; the* QUEEN *rakes in her tricks; in the last round but one the* KING *throws away the ace of Diamonds instead of the ace of Clubs, thereby enabling* CATHERINE *to make the King of Diamonds.*

THE QUEEN (*triumphantly*). The Grand Slam!

THE DAUPHIN. You wouldn't have made it if Papa had played properly, and not thrown away his ace of Diamonds.

THE KING. I couldn't have done anything else, and it wouldn't have made the slightest difference.

THE DAUPHIN. We should have saved the slam, that's all.

THE KING. In the first place you ought never to have redoubled.

THE DAUPHIN. I held excellent cards.

THE KING. You had nothing at all—absolutely nothing.

THE DAUPHIN. Two aces; ace, King, Knave, ten of Clubs——

THE KING. I had the ten of Clubs.

CATHERINE. No, papa, I had the ten.

THE DAUPHIN. I'm quite positive I had the ten.

THE QUEEN. As a matter of fact I had the ten of Clubs.

THE KING. I know I had the ten. It's not the slightest use discussing the matter.

CATHERINE. Oh, Papa, how can you say that? Of course you hadn't.

THE KING. I played this game before you were born, and I suppose I know if a hand is a no-trumper or not.

THE DAUPHIN. I had a much better hand than Catherine's. She had no right to double.

CATHERINE. I had everything——

THE DAUPHIN. Besides which it wasn't fair.

CATHERINE. What wasn't fair?

THE DAUPHIN. To play Hearts.

THE KING. You're quite right, Charles, it wasn't fair.

THE DAUPHIN. You would never have played Hearts, if Mamma hadn't told you to.

THE QUEEN. I never told the child anything. I only played according to the rules.

THE KING. In the first place the rule didn't apply, and in the second place it's not the rule. It's a stupid convention invented by the Italians.

THE QUEEN. I always have played Hearts in doubled no trumps, and I always shall.

THE KING. You might just as well give your partner a kick under the table.

CATHERINE. I should have played Hearts in any case.

THE DAUPHIN. What a lie!

CATHERINE. It's you who tell lies. You said you'd the ten of Clubs.

THE DAUPHIN. We've always played from the shortest suit before.

THE KING. Besides which, you never said a word about it until you saw your cards.

THE QUEEN. Of course not, because I always play Hearts. It's so much the best game.

THE KING. If you did that with other people they'd consider it cheating.

THE DAUPHIN. It was cheating.

CATHERINE. You needn't talk about cheating,

Charles. You cheated this morning at tennis—twice.

THE DAUPHIN. I didn't. You don't understand the score. No woman does.

THE KING. Women have got no morals about cards whatsoever.

THE QUEEN. As a matter of fact we should have won anyhow, if Catherine had played Hearts or not.

CATHERINE. Of course we should.

THE DAUPHIN. Oh! Really!

THE KING. You couldn't possibly have made the odd trick.

THE QUEEN. We should have made at least four tricks; we couldn't help it.

THE KING. And you talk the whole time—no wonder one loses.

THE DAUPHIN. It's quite impossible to play when they interrupt.

THE KING. And touch the cards.

THE Dauphin. And tell each other what to play.

THE KING. And argue about every trick.

THE DAUPHIN. And then never tell the truth.

THE QUEEN. If I were you, Charles, I would learn the rudimentary elements of the game.

THE KING. And not double when you've got nothing.

CATHERINE. And not revoke.

THE DAUPHIN. When did I revoke?

CATHERINE. Last night.

THE DAUPHIN. I didn't.

CATHERINE. I suppose it wasn't a real revoke, just like I suppose you had the ten of Clubs just now.

THE DAUPHIN. So I had.

CATHERINE. You wouldn't dare play like that if we were playing for money.

THE DAUPHIN. Very well. If you think I cheat I shan't play at all.

[*He goes out of the room and slams the door.*

THE KING. We'll play without him.

CATHERINE. I'd much rather play without him. Charles is quite impossible at cards—in fact at all games.

THE QUEEN. Whose deal is it?

THE KING. We must begin a fresh rubber. When one plays three, a game counts for a rubber.

THE QUEEN. Charles!

THE DAUPHIN (*opening the door*). What is it?

THE QUEEN. Come back at once. Don't be so silly. Your father wants to play.

THE DAUPHIN. It's no good my playing if you all say I cheat.

CATHERINE. I never said you cheated.

THE QUEEN. Come back directly. (*The* DAUPHIN *comes back and sits down at the table sulkily.*)

THE KING. Whose deal is it?

CATHERINE. Mine.

THE DAUPHIN. Mine.

CATHERINE. Papa dealt last time.

THE DAUPHIN. No; you dealt and I doubled.

CATHERINE. Papa dealt and left it.

THE DAUPHIN. You dealt, because I remember you nearly made a misdeal.

CATHERINE. I never make misdeals.

THE DAUPHIN. Always.

CATHERINE. Very well. You'd better play without me.

[*She goes out and slams the door.*

THE KING. Oh, dear! Oh, dear! They'll drive me mad!

THE QUEEN (*going to the door*). Catherine, come back this moment. Because Charles chooses to make a fool of himself that's no reason why you should.

CATHERINE. I don't want to play. It's no fun playing with Charles.

THE KING. Oh! do let's go on with the game. Do try not to quarrel so, children. (CATHERINE *comes back and sits down.*)

CATHERINE. I'll come back this time, but if he says I cheat again, I shall never play again as long as I live.

THE QUEEN. Hush! It's Catherine's deal.

CATHERINE. There, you see!

THE QUEEN. Hush!

[CATHERINE *deals.*

THE QUEEN (*looking at her cards*). I shouldn't at all mind if it was left to me this time.

THE KING. You've no business whatever to say a word.

THE QUEEN. As if it made any difference!

THE KING. It makes an enormous difference.

THE QUEEN. Not in this case.

THE KING. That's nothing to do with it. It's the principle that's wrong.

CATHERINE. I leave it.

THE KING. There you see!

CATHERINE. Papa, I couldn't do anything else.

THE QUEEN. I make no trumps.

[*The* DAUPHIN *leads a card; the* QUEEN *puts down her cards, revealing an excellent lead;* CATHERINE *hesitates a moment what to play from dummy's hand, the* QUEEN *touches one of dummy's cards to show.*

THE KING. Isabeau, the dummy has no business to touch the cards. That *is* cheating if you like.

THE QUEEN (*rising up in great dignity*). I've played cards for twenty-five years and have never yet been called a cheat in my own house.

[*She walks to the door.*

CATHERINE. Mamma, Mamma, do come back.

THE DAUPHIN (*walking after her*). Oh! Do come back !

THE KING (*getting up*). Don't be so absurd. You're all of you one worse than the other !

THE QUEEN. No, no, he called me a cheat.

THE KING. I never did anything of the sort.

THE QUEEN. No wonder the children never speak the truth when they've got such a father !

THE KING. Now sit down and let's go on.

[*They sit down. The* KING *plays.* CATHERINE *plays from her hand, and then the* DAUPHIN. CATHERINE *again hestitates about dummy's card, and the* QUEEN *again touches a card showing her what to play.*

THE DAUPHIN. Papa, Mamma's cheated again.

THE QUEEN (*getting up*). I won't have you say that.

CATHERINE (*shouting*). Oh! Charles !

THE DAUPHIN (*screaming*). But she showed you——

[*The* KING *gets up and throws the cards to the other end of the room, kicks over the card-table, and rushes to the door screaming.*

THE QUEEN (*terror-stricken*). Heaven have mercy upon us, your father's gone mad !

CURTAIN.

VII

THE REHEARSAL

SCENE.—*The Globe Theatre*, 1595. *On the stage the* AUTHOR, *the* PRODUCER, *and the* STAGE MANAGER *are standing. A rehearsal of " Macbeth " is about to begin. Waiting in the wings are the actors who are playing the* WITCHES, BANQUO, MACDUFF, *etc. They are all men.*

THE STAGE MANAGER. We'd better begin with the last act.

THE PRODUCER. I think we'll begin with the first act. We've never done it all through yet.

THE STAGE MANAGER. Mr. Colman isn't here. It's no good doing the first act without Duncan.

THE PRODUCER. Where is Mr. Colman? Did you let him know about rehearsal?

THE STAGE MANAGER. I sent a messenger to his house in Gray's Inn.

THE FIRST WITCH. Mr. Colman is playing Psyche in a masque at Kenilworth. He won't be back until the day after to-morrow.

THE PRODUCER. That settles it. We'll begin with the fifth act.

THE FIRST WITCH. Then I suppose I can go.

THE SECOND WITCH. } And I suppose we
THE THIRD WITCH } needn't wait.

THE STAGE MANAGER. Certainly not. We're going on to the fourth act as soon as we've done the fifth.

BANQUO. But I suppose you don't want me.

THE STAGE MANAGER. And what about your ghost entrance in Act IV? We must get the business right this time; besides, we'll do the second act if we've time. Now, Act V, Mr. Thomas and Mr. Bowles, please.

THE FIRST WITCH. Mr. Bowles can't come to-day. He told me to tell you. He's having a tooth pulled out.

THE STAGE MANAGER. Then will you read the waiting gentlewoman's part, Mr. Lyle. You can take this scrip.

[*The* FIRST WITCH *takes the scrip.*

Where is Mr. Thomas?

THE FIRST WITCH. He said he was coming.

THE STAGE MANAGER. We can't wait. I'll read his part. We'll leave out the beginning and just give Mr. Hughes his cue.

THE FIRST WITCH (*reading*). " Having no witness to confirm my speech."

THE STAGE MANAGER. Mr. HUGHES.

THE FIRST WITCH. He was here a moment ago.

THE STAGE MANAGER (*louder*). Mr. Hughes.

Enter LADY MACBETH (MR. HUGHES, *a young man about* 24)

LADY MACBETH. Sorry. (*He comes on down some steps L.C.*)

THE PRODUCER. That will never do, Mr. Hughes; there's no necessity to sway as if you were intoxicated, and you mustn't look at your feet.

LADY MACBETH. It's the steps. They're so rickety.

THE PRODUCER. We'll begin again from " speech."

[LADY MACBETH *comes on again. He looks straight in front of him and falls heavily on to the ground.*

I said those steps were to be mended yesterday.

[*The* FIRST WITCH *is convulsed with laughter.*

LADY MACBETH. There's nothing to laugh at.

THE PRODUCER. Are you hurt, Mr. Hughes?

LADY MACBETH. Not much. (*The steps are replaced by two supers.*)

THE PRODUCER. Now from " speech."

[MR. HUGHES *comes on again.*

THE PRODUCER. You must not hold the taper upside down.

LADY MACBETH. How can I rub my hands and hold a taper too? What's the use of the taper?

THE PRODUCER. You can rub the back of your hand. You needn't wash your hands in the air. That's better.

[*The dialogue between the* DOCTOR *and the* GENTLE-WOMAN *proceeds until* LADY MACBETH'S *cue:* " *hour.*"

Enter the DOCTOR (Mr. THOMAS). *He waits R.*

LADY MACBETH. " Here's a damned spot."

THE STAGE MANAGER. No, no, Mr. Hughes, " Yet here's a spot."

THE PRODUCER. Begin again from " hands."

GENTLEWOMAN. " It is an accustomed action with her, to seem thus washing her hands. I've known her to continue in this three-quarters of an hour."

LADY MACBETH. " Yet here's a damned spot."

THE STAGE MANAGER. It's not " damned " at all. That comes later.

LADY MACBETH. It's catchy. Couldn't I say " mark " instead of " spot " in the first line?

THE DOCTOR (*coming forward*). That would entirely spoil the effect of my " Hark ! " You see " mark " rhymes with " Hark." It's impossible.

THE PRODUCER. Oh ! It's you, Mr. Thomas. Will you go straight on. We'll do the whole scene over presently. Now from " hour."

LADY MACBETH. " Yes, here's a spot."

THE STAGE MANAGER. It's not " Yes," but " Yet," Mr. Hughes.

LADY MACBETH. " Yet here's a spot."

THE DOCTOR (*at the top of his voice*) " Hark ! "

THE PRODUCER. Not so loud, Mr. Thomas, that would wake her up.

THE DOCTOR (*in a high falsetto*). " Har-r-rk ! She spe-e-e-aks. I will . . . set . . . down."

THE PRODUCER. You needn't bleat that " speaks," Mr. Thomas, and the second part of that line is cut.

THE DOCTOR. It's not cut in my part. " Hark, she speaks."

LADY MACBETH. " Yet here's a spot."

THE STAGE MANAGER. No, Mr. Hughes; " out damned spot."

LADY MACBETH. Sorry.

THE PRODUCER. We must get that right. Now from " hour."

LADY MACBETH. " Yet here's a spot."

THE DOCTOR. " Hark ! she speaks."

LADY MACBETH. " Get out, damned spot ! Get out, I say ! One, two, three, four : why there's plenty of time to do't. Oh ! Hell ! Fie, fie, my Lord ! a soldier and a beard ! What have we got to fear when none can call our murky power to swift account withal ? You'd never have thought the old man had so much blood in him ! "

THE AUTHOR. I don't think you've got those lines quite right yet, Mr. Hughes.

LADY MACBETH. What's wrong ?

THE STAGE MANAGER. There's no " get." It's " one; two " : and not " one, two, three, four." Then it's " Hell is murky." And there's no " plenty." And it's " a soldier and *afeared*," and not " a soldier and a *beard*."

THE AUTHOR. And after that you made two lines into rhymed verse.

MR. HUGHES. Yes, I know I did. I thought it wanted it.

THE PRODUCER. Please try to speak your lines as they are written, Mr. Hughes.

Enter MR. BURBAGE, *who plays Macbeth.*

MR. BURBAGE. That scene doesn't go. Now don't you think Macbeth had better walk in his sleep instead of Lady Macbeth ?

THE STAGE MANAGER. That's an idea.

THE PRODUCER. I think the whole scene might be cut. It's quite unnecessary.

LADY MACBETH. Then I shan't come on in the whole of the fifth act. If that scene's cut I shan't play at all.

THE STAGE MANAGER. We're thinking of trans-

ferring the scene to Macbeth. (*To the* AUTHOR.)
It wouldn't need much altering. Would you mind
rewriting that scene, Mr. Shakespeare? It wouldn't
want much alteration. You'd have to change that
line about Arabia. Instead of this " little hand,"
you might say : " All the perfumes of Arabia will
not sweeten this horny hand." I'm not sure it isn't
more effective.

THE AUTHOR. I'm afraid it might get a laugh.

MR. BURBAGE. Not if I play it.

THE AUTHOR. I think it's more likely that Lady
Macbeth would walk in her sleep, but——

MR. BURBAGE. That doesn't signify. I can make
a great hit in that scene.

LADY MACBETH. If you take that scene from me,
I shan't play Juliet to-night.

THE STAGE MANAGER (*aside to* PRODUCER). We
can't possibly get another Juliet.

THE PRODUCER. On the whole, I think we must
leave the scene as it is.

MR. BURBAGE. I've got nothing to do in the last
act. What's the use of my coming to rehearsal when
there's nothing for me to rehearse?

THE PRODUCER. Very well, Mr. Burbage. We'll
go on to the Third Scene at once. We'll go through
your scene again later, Mr. Hughes.

MR. BURBAGE. Before we do this scene there's a
point I wish to settle. In Scene V, when Seyton
tells me the Queen's dead, I say : " She should
have died hereafter ; there would have been a time
for such a word " ; and then the messenger enters.
I should like a soliloquy here, about twenty or thirty
lines, if possible in rhyme, in any case ending with
a tag. I should like it to be about Lady Macbeth.

Macbeth might have something touching to say about their happy domestic life, and the early days of their marriage. He might refer to their courtship. I must have something to make Macbeth sympathetic, otherwise the public won't stand it. He might say his better-half had left him, and then he might refer to her beauty. The speech might begin :

> O dearest chuck, it is unkind indeed
> To leave me in the midst of my sore need.

Or something of the kind. In any case it ought to rhyme. Could I have that written at once, and then we could rehearse it ?

THE PRODUCER. Certainly, certainly, Mr. Burbage. Will you write it yourself, Mr. Shakespeare, or shall we get some one else to do it ?

THE AUTHOR. I'll do it myself if some one will read my part.

THE PRODUCER. Let me see; I forget what is your part.

THE STAGE MANAGER. Mr. Shakespeare is playing Seyton. (*Aside.*) We cast him for Duncan, but he wasn't up to it.

THE PRODUCER. Mr. Kydd, will you read Mr. Shakespeare's part ?

BANQUO. Certainly.

THE PRODUCER. Please let us have that speech, Mr. Shakespeare, as quickly as possible. (*Aside.*) Don't make it too long. Ten lines at the most.

THE AUTHOR (*aside*). Is it absolutely necessary that it should rhyme ?

THE PRODUCER (*aside*). No, of course not; that's Burbage's fad.

[*Exit the* AUTHOR *into the wings.*

MR. BURBAGE. I should like to go through the fight first.

THE PRODUCER. Very well, Mr. Burbage.

THE STAGE MANAGER. Macduff—Mr. Foote——

MACDUFF. I'm here.

MR. BURBAGE. I'll give you the cue :
" Why should I play the fool and like a Roman
  Die on my sword, while there is life, there's hope;
  The gashes are for them."

MACDUFF. " Turn, hell-hound, turn."

MR. BURBAGE. I don't think Macduff ought to call Macbeth a hell-hound.

THE PRODUCER. What do you suggest?

MR. BURBAGE. I should suggest : " False Monarch, turn." It's more dignified.

MACDUFF. I would rather say " hell-hound."

THE PRODUCER. Supposing we make it " King of Hell."

MR. BURBAGE. I don't think that would do

THE PRODUCER. Then we must leave it for the present.

MACDUFF. " Turn, hell-hound, turn."

[*They begin to fight with wooden swords.*

THE STAGE MANAGER. You don't begin to fight till Macduff says " Give thee out."

MR. BURBAGE. I think we might run those two speeches into one, and I might say :
" Of all men I would have avoided thee,
  But come on now, although my soul is charged
  With blood of thine, I'll have no further words.
  My voice is in my sword."
Then Macduff could say :
" O bloodier villain than terms can well express."

THE PRODUCER. We must consult the author about that.

MR. BURBAGE. We'll do the fencing without words first.

[*They begin to fight again.* MACDUFF *gives* MR. BURBAGE *a tremendous blow on the shoulder.*

MR. BURBAGE. Oh! oh! That's my rheumatic shoulder. Please be a little more careful, Mr. Foote. You know I've got no padding. I can't go on rehearsing now. I am very seriously hurt indeed.

MACDUFF. I'm sure I'm very sorry. It was entirely an accident.

MR. BURBAGE. I'm afraid I must go home. I don't feel up to it.

THE STAGE MANAGER. I'll send for some ointment. Please be more careful, Mr. Foote. Couldn't you possibly see your way to take Scene III, Mr. Burbage?

MR. BURBAGE. I know Scene III backwards. However, I'll just run through my speech.

THE STAGE MANAGER. What? "This push will cheer me ever"?

MR. BURBAGE (*peevishly*). No, not that one. You know that's all right. That tricky speech about medicine. Give me the cue.

THE STAGE MANAGER. "That keep her from her rest."

MR. BURBAGE.   " Cure her of that :
Canst thou not minister to a sickly mind,
Pull from the memory a rooted sorrow,
Rub out the troubles of the busy brain,
And with a sweet and soothing antidote
Clean the stiff bosom of that dangerous poison
Which weighs upon the heart? "
There, you see, word-perfect. What did I say?

THE STAGE MANAGER. Yes, yes, Mr. Burbage. Here's Mr. Shakespeare.

THE AUTHOR. I've written that speech. Shall I read it?

THE PRODUCER. Please.

MR. SHAKESPEARE (*reads*). " To-morrow, and to-morrow, and to-morrow,
Creeps in this petty pace from day to day,
To the last syllable of recorded time;
And all our yesterdays have lighted fools
The way to dusty death. Out, out, brief candle!
Life's but a walking shadow, a poor player
That struts and frets his hour upon the stage,
And then is heard no more; it is a tale
Told by an idiot, full of sound and fury,
Signifying nothing."

MR. BURBAGE. Well, you don't expect me to say that, I suppose. It's a third too short. There's not a single rhyme in it. It's got nothing to do with the situation, and it's an insult to the stage. " Struts and frets " indeed! I see there's nothing left for me but to throw up the part. You can get any one you please to play Macbeth. One thing is quite certain, I won't. [*Exit* MR. BURBAGE *in a passion.*

THE STAGE MANAGER (*to the* AUTHOR). Now you've done it.

THE AUTHOR (*to the* PRODUCER). You said it needn't rhyme.

THE PRODUCER. It's Macduff. It was all your fault, Mr. Foote.

LADY MACBETH. Am I to wear a fair wig or a dark wig?

THE PRODUCER. Oh! I don't know.

THE AUTHOR. Dark, if you please. People are

always saying I'm making portraits. So, if you're dark, nobody can say I meant the character for the Queen or for Mistress Mary Fytton.

THE STAGE MANAGER. It's no good going on now. It's all up—it's all up.

CURTAIN.

VIII

THE BLUE HARLEQUIN

(WITH APOLOGIES TO MR. MAETERLINCK)

SCENE.—*A London street; the houses are scarcely visible in the diaphanous mist. On the right, darkling, is a sausage shop; on the left a greengrocer's. The shop windows glimmer like opals.*

Enter a POLICEMAN. *He is dressed in a cerulean tunic, and his truncheon is transparent and glows like a beryl.*

THE POLICEMAN. It was not on my beat. It was not on my beat.

Enter the PANTALOON. *He is very old.*

THE PANTALOON. I am very old. I am so old that I cannot remember things. I cannot remember names.

THE POLICEMAN. Move on.

THE PANTALOON. I am always moving on. I feel like a sea-gull.

THE POLICEMAN. Move on. I have already told you to move on.

THE PANTALOON. He told me to move on. He said I would be obliged to move on. I am so old that I forget what they say to me.

THE POLICEMAN. Your beard is like grass. It is like the grass that grows over men's graves. I do not like your beard.

THE PANTALOON. You have no beard. Your face is smooth. It has a hole on one side of it like a cheese. The moon has a hole on one side of it. It is foggy in the street.

[*Pointing to the door of the sausage shop.* Behind that door there is no fog.

THE POLICEMAN. Nobody has ever opened that door. The key of that door is lost. The lock is broken. It is a useless door.

THE PANTALOON. Years ago that door had a key. There was a little red stain on the key. It wanted cleaning.

THE POLICEMAN. It was a rusty key.

THE PANTALOON. It was a latch-key.

THE POLICEMAN. It was lost on a Thursday.

THE PANTALOON. On the Friday they came to clean the key, but it was too dark to clean it.

THE POLICEMAN. On Saturday morning there was no time. On Saturday afternoon the shops were shut.

THE PANTALOON. The shops were shut all Sunday.

THE POLICEMAN. Monday was Bank Holiday. They went away on Monday.

THE PANTALOON. It rained all day on Monday. It poured with rain. The rain was damp. It had come from a damp place. It was wet rain.

THE POLICEMAN. They told me he was wanted.

THE PANTALOON. They asked me what time it was. I said : "I am so old I have forgotten what time it is. I cannot remember things."

THE POLICEMAN. They came back on Monday night. When they came back they had forgotten all about the key.

THE PANTALOON. I said if you want to know what time it is you must ask the policeman. The policeman knows.

THE POLICEMAN. He knows.

THE PANTALOON. What time is it?

THE POLICEMAN. It is seven minutes to five. It will soon be five minutes to five.

THE PANTALOON. She goes out at five, every day, for a walk.

THE POLICEMAN. She will walk through the fog at five. She is sure to come. I am certain she will come.

THE PANTALOON. She will tell him he is wanted.

THE POLICEMAN If he comes on to my beat I will take up him.

THE PANTALOON. He will never come on to your beat.

Enter the CLOWN *with a red-hot poker,
which shines like a carbuncle*

THE CLOWN. It is strange that we should meet here again. We always meet at the same place and at the same hour.

THE PANTALOON. I am so old I had forgotten I should meet you. When you walked down the street I thought you were some one else. I thought I had never seen you before.

THE CLOWN. It is so foggy in the street and my poker is getting cold.

THE PANTALOON. If you put it in the fire it will get warm again.

THE CLOWN. There is no fire in the street. The policeman says we may not light a fire in the street. It is dangerous. It frightens the people.

THE PANTALOON. Last time they lit a fire in the street it was the 5th of November.

THE CLOWN. The policeman was not there on the 5th of November.

THE PANTALOON. It was not on his beat.

THE CLOWN. His beat is far away—on the sand.

THE PANTALOON. There is a cave near his beat.

THE CLOWN. There is a public-house near his beat. There is a public-house quite close to his beat. It has two doors.

THE PANTALOON. One is marked " Public." He never opens that door.

THE CLOWN. The other is marked " Private." He opens it and it swings backwards and forwards.

THE PANTALOON. The people inside complain of the draught. They are always complaining.

THE CLOWN. She waits for him on the other side of the railings.

THE PANTALOON. The railings are very strong. They are black railings. They are in front of the area. She hands things to him through the railings. She gives him things to eat and things to drink.

THE CLOWN. It is on his beat.

THE PANTALOON. No, it is not on his beat, but it is quite close to his beat. Your poker has got cold.

THE CLOWN. I will warm it. I will warm it on the back of the policeman. He has a broad back.

[*He rubs the* POLICEMAN *with the poker.*

THE POLICEMAN. That poker is warm. It is

much warmer than you think it is. (*The* CLOWN *rubs him again.*) When you do that I feel strange. I feel as if a ruby were burning near me.

THE CLOWN. I am warming you with my poker. It is good to be warm. It is so cold in this street. It never used to be so cold. It is foggy. The fog makes me hungry and thirsty. I am so hungry that I would like to eat a sausage.

THE PANTALOON. I am so hungry that I would like to eat many sausages, first one and then another. I could eat six sausages.

THE CLOWN. Let us go and take some sausages. There are some sausages hanging in that shop. I cannot see them through the fog, but I know there are some sausages there.

THE PANTALOON. I can see the sausages. They are all huddled together like pigeons.

THE CLOWN. They are close together like little wood-pigeons. I like sausages. But before we go I will warm the policeman. He is so cold.

THE PANTALOON. It is not on his beat.

[*The* CLOWN *rubs the* POLICEMAN *with his poker.*

THE POLICEMAN. When you do that I feel as if this had happened before. I feel as if I were in a strange room full of doors and lighted candles. I do not like the feeling.

[*The* PANTALOON *and the* CLOWN *go into the sausage shop.*

Enter COLUMBINE

COLUMBINE. I had nine sisters. They were all blind, and they were all born on a Friday. Friday is an unlucky day.

THE POLICEMAN. I have been waiting for you. I thought you had gone to him. He is wanted. I thought you had gone to tell him he is wanted.

COLUMBINE. You will never find him.

THE POLICEMAN. I have been looking for him since Wednesday. I am tired of looking. It was not on my beat.

COLUMBINE. You will never find him. He knows you are looking for him. When he sees you coming round the corner of the street he runs away round the other corner. He runs quicker than you. Nobody runs so quickly as he does.

THE POLICEMAN. I saw the end of his wand yesterday. It was quite white. It was as white as the milk in the pails.

COLUMBINE. The milk in the pails is not always white. Sometimes it is yellow. But his wand is white. He hits people with it and he runs away. He runs so fast nobody can catch him.

THE POLICEMAN. I saw the spangles of his clothes the day before yesterday. They were all gold. I looked again and I thought they were silver spangles. I thought his clothes were red at first. Afterwards they seemed to be green as leaves in the orchard they cut down.

COLUMBINE. Why did they cut it down?

THE POLICEMAN. Because it was green. There are too many green orchards.

COLUMBINE. He changes his clothes so quickly nobody knows what he has got on.

THE POLICEMAN. His clothes are like the scales of fishes. They are like the scales of grey fishes in the old pond. The old pond is full of fishes. It ought to be dredged.

F

COLUMBINE. Nobody will ever dredge the old pond. The children fish in it.

THE POLICEMAN. His clothes are like the wings of birds. Like the wings of owls, that fly about in the tower, hooting. The tower is full of owls. It ought to be pulled down.

COLUMBINE. Nobody will ever pull down the tower. The owls kill the mice.

THE POLICEMAN. His clothes are like red sparks. Like the sparks that fly from the horses' hoofs in the crooked lane. The crooked lane is full of horses. It ought to be made into a field.

COLUMBINE. It will never be made into a field. Too many people use the crooked lane. It leads to the mill. It is the shortest way to the mill.

THE POLICEMAN. His clothes are like the blue pebbles the old women drop into the stream. The stream is full of pebbles. It ought to be dried up.

COLUMBINE. It will never be dried up, because the old women wash their clothes in it. It is not pebbles they throw into it. It is blue from the blue-bag. They throw it in to whiten the linen.

THE POLICEMAN. I do not know. It is not on my beat. Some people say it is pebbles. Their linen is all in holes. It is frayed linen.

COLUMBINE. His linen is never frayed.

THE POLICEMAN. His clothes hide his linen. You cannot tell what colour his clothes are. Sometimes they are blue and sometimes they are red.

COLUMBINE. Some people say they are grey clothes—grey like the sand.

THE POLICEMAN. They told me they were blue. I am sure his clothes are blue.

Enter the CLOWN *through the window*

THE CLOWN. I would have brought you some sausages. I would have brought you a hundred sausages. They are made of pork. The pig was killed on a Friday.

COLUMBINE. Everything always happens on a Friday. I was born on a Friday.

THE CLOWN. I would have brought you more sausages than I can eat myself. I would have brought you more sausages than you can eat.

THE POLICEMAN. Nobody can eat more than a certain amount of sausages. That is why they are so sad in this street. I can eat a great many sausages.

COLUMBINE. It is a bad thing to eat too many sausages.

THE CLOWN. It is not right to go into a shop, to take away the sausages, and to eat them. The shopkeeper called him a thief because he took away the sausages.

THE POLICEMAN. It is not on my beat.

COLUMBINE. He was very hungry.

THE CLOWN. He had no right to take away all the sausages. There were none left for us. If he had not taken away all the sausages I could have brought them to you. He jumped down the chimney. It was cleaned yesterday. He took away all the sausages. He took away the sausages I would have brought you. I had meant to bring them all.

THE POLICEMAN. What colour were his clothes?

THE CLOWN. I was so frightened when he took away the sausages that I did not notice the colour of his clothes. I think they were red clothes.

THE POLICEMAN. Were they not blue clothes?

THE CLOWN. They may have been blue clothes.

He jumped down the chimney and drew out his knife.
It was a steel knife, and there were spots on the blade.
He cut the string of the sausages from the ceiling.
They were all huddled together in the ceiling like
birds . . . like birds in the winter.

Enter the PANTALOON

THE PANTALOON. He has taken away all the
sausages. I was going to bring you sausages to eat.
They were hanging from the roof like little fat mice.
But I am so old—I forget things. Then he came
with his knife and cut them down. You must take
him up. He has stolen the sausages. They were
not his sausages.

THE POLICEMAN. It is not on my beat. What
colour were his clothes?

THE PANTALOON. I am so old I forget things. I
think they were green clothes.

THE POLICEMAN. Were they not blue clothes?

THE CLOWN (to the POLICEMAN). You are so cold.
I will warm you with my poker. It is a red-hot
poker.

THE POLICEMAN. Whenever you do that I feel
strange.   [The CLOWN rubs him with the poker.

THE POLICEMAN. I will take away your poker.
I do not like to be made to feel strange so often.

[The CLOWN runs away and jumps through the
shop window. The POLICEMAN runs after him.
At that moment the HARLEQUIN—he is all blue
—darts round the street corner and runs off
with COLUMBINE.

THE POLICEMAN. He has run away with her
They said he would come when I was not looking.

I shall never catch him. His clothes were blue. (*To the* PANTALOON) I will take you up instead. I will say you took the sausages. I will not speak the truth. You will speak the truth. You will say he took the sausages. But they will not believe you. They will believe me. Now you shall come with me, along.

THE PANTALOON. I am so old. I feel as if all this had happened before.

THE POLICEMAN. I will say it was on my beat.

> [*As he leads off the* PANTALOON, *the* CLOWN *jumps out of the window and hits him with the red-hot poker.*

THE POLICEMAN. Whenever he does that I feel strange.

> [*The* PANTALOON *escapes and fades into the fog.*

CURTAIN.

IX

THE MEMBER FOR LITERATURE

*It having been settled that a Member for " Literature "
should be elected to the House of Commons, a plebis-
cite was taken among the members of all the literary
clubs and societies in London.*

*The result was that Mr. M—x B—b—m, Mr. H—ll
C—e, Mr. R—d—d K—p—g, and Mr. J—e
K. J—e all received exactly the same number of
votes. In order to settle which of them should be
chosen, it was decided that these four authors should
each in turn address the same public meeting,
after which the election should be by ballot, and the
author chosen by the audience at the meeting should
be the Member for Literature.*

SCENE.—*A hall at Battersea. On the platform are a*
CHAIRMAN, *a small Committee, and the four* AUTHORS
in question.

Mr. M—x B—b—m (*rises to address the meeting*).
No politician I.

A VOICE FROM THE BACK OF THE HALL. Then why
the —— —— do you come here to talk politics?

Mr. M—x B—b—m. That, gentle public, is what
I wish carefully to avoid doing. You can lead me
to the hustings, but you cannot make me think

—politically. Therefore bear with me a little. Examine yourselves and you will see that, were you in my position, you would do exactly what I am going to do now. Candidature has been thrust upon me. I am forced to speak to you, I am indeed anxious to speak to you so that you may be able to choose one of the three distinguished literary men, whom you see before you on this platform, to be your Literary Member, and I wish to prevent your choice falling upon me.

I will put before you in chosen sentences, which I have carefully arranged beforehand, the reasons why I think you should not elect me. I do not want to be elected. To elect me would indeed be an unfriendly act. Such a choice would not only cause me inconvenience, but it would bring to yourselves neither profit nor pleasure. Be sure I should never think of your interests, be surer still I should never attend the tedious sittings at St. Stephen's. I have listened to eloquence at the Oxford Union and to the gentle rhetoric of Cambridge. Not for me are the efforts of the half-witted and the wholly inarticulate at Westminster, who stammer where old Gladstone used to sing. If you have views I am not privy to them, and from your sympathies I am aloof. I know well enough that you—no more than I—care a red farthing whether the label of your Member be Liberal or Conservative. What you do care for, and what leaves me frigid, is the figure whom you can encourage by chaff or vex by sarcasm.

You want to hear that Lloyd George ought to be thrown into a den of Suffragettes—(*Hear, Hear*)— or that Winston Churchill is good and old. (*Hear, Hear.*) You want to hear it not adumbrated, but said emphatically and without the introduction of a *nuance*, either that Mr. Balfour is infallible or that he is invincibly ignorant. (*Cheers and groans.*)

Now, I care not whether Mr. Balfour be right or wrong. I murmur to myself the jest of Pilate, and I do not wait for the answer. And as to the province of affairs which concerns you here, the province of the Budget, the Fiscal Question, Home Rule, the House of Lords, the Disestablishment of the Welsh Church, and other fallalas, it is for me a vague land into which Leonardo da Vinci never looked forward, and about which I have not experienced the least curiosity; nor do I care whether Mr. Balfour be inspired by an angel or an ape. (*Liberal cheers.*)

As to Mr. Asquith's claims, I am just as undecided and just as indifferent. (*Conservative cheers.*) I know nothing about the Education Bill or the Children's Bill; I have heard that one of these measures will make " Hunt the Slipper " compulsory for children under five years old, and that there is somewhere a clause being moulded which will prevent boys over sixteen years of age from playing marbles in the public thoroughfares. But since before long children will have votes for themselves and be represented in Parliament—(*cries of " Votes for Children "*) —we can surely for the present leave these perplexing questions gently suspended until they shall be dealt with by those whom they more nearly concern. (*A little boy is carried out struggling and waving a megaphone.*)

But you will say—our Imperial Policy? Well, I will be frank, I am in favour of the restoration of the Heptarchy. Had I my way even Rutland should have, not only Home Rule—(*Liberal cheers*)

—but a King, by Divine Right absolute. Of course, I wish our present King to remain a super-King of all the little Englands, of the 52 (or is it 365?) counties of England. (*Loud cheers.*) As for the Colonies, blood may be thicker than water, but water, happily for us, is broader than blood— (*loud cheers*)—and I have always been thankful that we are separated from America, and from our other high-spirited offsprings, by so broad an ocean as the Atlantic. Our Colonies are our children. Their place is in the nursery or at school. There let us leave them to their ninepins, their whipping-tops, their rocking-horses, and their marbles. Their exploits can only weary us who are their grown-up parents, we who are obliged to read their tri-monthly reports, and to pay wages which we can ill afford for their nurses and their ushers.

I hear a lady murmuring the words " Budget " and " Fiscal Question "—magical words, it is true. But we need hardly discuss them, because whatever we say or do there will always be a Budget; there will always be a Fiscal Question, and a vague alternative to it preached by an indignant and sanguine Opposition.

Whatever our taxes may be, and however we have to pay them, they will always have to be paid, and I for one shall never pay them with ecstasy. (*Cheers.*) Formerly the poor had the exclusive right of paying taxes; now it is rumoured that the rich have usurped that privilege, and so grossly abused it that, the rich having become poorer than the poor, the poor must needs pay a super-tax. (*Groans and cries of " Shame."*) Well, I only desire that there may always be people so much richer than myself that they will pay me cheerfully and generously for taking pains to write what few will trouble to read. When the day comes that there will be no more rich—(Oh, dreadful day !) —Max's occupation will be gone, because even were I then to draw flaming seascapes in coloured chalk on the paving-stones of Piccadilly, there will be no one richer than myself to drop a bad halfpenny into the saucer which shall hang under the card, so needlessly telling the passer-by what the pictures themselves proclaim : that the artist is blind.

I think I have now lightly shaken by the hand the questions which, as the phrase goes, are at issue, and although I have not given you my reasons in clauses, headings, and sections, I hope I have made it perspicuous to you that I do not wish to be a member of Parliament, and that were I to be chosen, I should not lift my eye-glass to justify your choice; I would not sacrifice the whiff of a cigarette for all the perfumes of St. Stephen's. But as a postscript, I am in favour of full-dress debates; and by that I mean debates in the House of Lords where the Peers are dressed in robe and coronet; and these debates, were I King of England, should be compulsory and frequent. And as one postscript leads to another, I will tell you that were a more competent Guy Fawkes to blow up the House of Commons, and were it never to arise from its ashes, I should say " Ouf ! "

[*He sits down. Discreet cheers.*

MR. H—LL C—E (*rises*). Mr. Chairman, ladies and gentlemen, loath as I have always been to obtrude upon the public gaze——

A VOICE. Why, it's Shakespeare !

ANOTHER VOICE. No, it tain't. It's the Wax Bust.

MR. H—LL C—E. Loath as I have always been——

A VOICE. As a Manxman, are you, or are you not, in favour of Votes for Women?

MR. H—LL C—E. Loath as I am——

THE SAME VOICE. He's not in favour of Votes for Women and he's a Manxman! (*A terrific blast is blown on toy trumpets and megaphones.*)

ANOTHER VOICE. Tails for Manx Cats.

MR. H—LL C—E. Loath as I am——

VOICES. Votes for Women. (*Loud uproar—some women are ejected.*)

[*After a hurried confabulation it is settled that MR. R—D—D K—P—G shall address the audience, and that MR. H—LL C—E shall speak later.*

MR. R—D—D K—P—G (*rises*). There was once an Aunt-Hill. It was a small Aunt-Hill, and from the summit to the base of it the distance was about as long as the slip of an E.P. Tent.

The Aunts were busy. They worked all day and sometimes all night. Now when Aunts work all night it's worth going to see. The hill grew bigger and bigger, and tunnels were burrowed, and after some months the Aunts had annexed a whole forest. They were pleased with themselves.

" The sun doesn't set on our Aunt-Hill," said one Aunt.

" Our Aunt-Hill is the key of the Eastern forest," said another. The Kingdom of the Aunts grew so large that they sent some of their younger workers to make Aunt-Hills beyond the forest. This they did, and their Aunt-Hills grew big, too. Then the

Aunts were pleased and said: " We are the greatest Aunts in the World." But one of the Aunts—he wrote things for the other Aunts to read—said: " Take care, you were small once; and if you don't go on working you'll be small again." But the Aunts said he was a fool. Then the Aunts began to get slack and look on at their little Aunts playing at rolling the acorn.

Now in a neighbouring forest a rival Aunt set up a hill and began training an army.

Then the Aunt who wrote things said: " Take care, these new Aunts will grow strong and take away your Aunt-Hill." But the Aunts didn't listen, they went on looking at the Aunts playing at rolling the acorn. And one of the leading Aunts said: " He's a scaremonger, don't listen. He's a ' Jing-aunt.' Its Unauntish to say such things." So nobody cared, and the new Aunts came and took the old Aunts' Aunt-Hill and made them all into slaves.

[MR. R—D—D K—P—G *sits down. (Cheers.)*

MR. J—E K. J—E (*rises*). Mr. Chairman, ladies and gentlemen——

A VOICE. Does your mother know you're out?

MR. J—E K. J—E. Yes, but my mother-in-law doesn't. (*Terrific cheers.*) Gentlemen, I don't think I need say any more. I'm the only man so far who has said to you a single word you've understood. (*Cheers.*) So I think I'll let well alone. My politics are Home Rule at Home, and down with Mothers-in-Law. (*Renewed cheering.*)

[MR. J—E K. J—E *sits down.*

[*After brief consultation on the platform,* MR. H—LL C—E *rises again.*

MR. H—LL C—E.   Loath as I am——
MANY WOMEN.   What about Votes for Women?

[*There is an uproar; a scuffle and a fight. It is impossible to continue the business, so the question as to who shall be elected is put to the Meeting. The people proceed to vote by ballot. The votes are then counted by the Committee in a room adjoining the platform. After an interval the* CHAIRMAN *comes on to the platform.*

THE CHAIRMAN. Ladies and gentlemen, I will now have the pleasure of reading out the result of the Election.   The figures are as follows :—

MR. J—E K. J—E (elected)	333
MR. R—D—D K—P—G	12
MR. M—X B—B—M	3
MR. H—LL C—E	2

[*The Meeting breaks up amidst terrific cheers.*

CURTAIN.

X

CALIGULA'S PICNIC

SCENE.—*A large banqueting table in the centre of a bridge, which stretches for three miles between Puteoli and Baiæ. The* EMPEROR CALIGULA *is reclining in the place of honour. There are hundreds of guests.*

RUFUS (*an intensely eager, bearded man to his neighbour* PROTEUS, *a dandy*). As I was saying, the whole point of the question is this: all diseases come from the secretion in the blood of certain poisons. Now since we imbibe these poisons from certain food-stuffs, what I say is—Cut off the poison at the supply.

PROTEUS (*helping himself to roast boar with stuffing*). Yes, yes, perfectly.

RUFUS. Cut off the poison at the supply. Prevent; don't try to cure when it's too late. You follow me?

PROTEUS (*absently*). Exactly. (*He gives himself an additional helping of roast boar.*)

RUFUS. But there you are, helping yourself to poison again. (RUFUS *gives up* PROTEUS *and turns to his other neighbour.*)

HYGERIUS (*on* PROTEUS's *right, an aged Senator*). May I trouble you for the peacock?

PROTEUS. I beg your pardon. (*He passes the peacock.*)

HYGERIUS. I suppose these peacocks are imported.

PROTEUS (*not interested*). I suppose so.

HYGERIUS. Now what I say is, the land's the question.

PROTEUS (*foreseeing a discourse on political economy*). The General is trying to catch your eye.

HYGERIUS. Where? Where? I don't see him.

PROTEUS. Right at the other end of the table. (*To his vis-à-vis*, DEMOPHILUS, *an officer*) Were you lucky yesterday?

DEMOPHILUS. No, I lost. They told me Chilon was a certainty.

PROTEUS. Ah! Chilon.

DEMOPHILUS. He didn't do himself justice.

PROTEUS. Over-trained?

HYGERIUS (*to his vis-à-vis*, PETRONIUS, *a fashionable philosopher*). Now you no doubt agree with me that nowadays the whole problem of agriculture——

PETRONIUS (*upsetting a large bowl of wine on the table on purpose*). A thousand pardons! It was too awkward of me.

[*Slaves come and mop up the mess.*

SEVERUS (*a literary man, sitting on* HYGERIUS's *left, to* PETRONIUS). " Spilt wine shall buy the favour of the Gods," as Particus says.

PETRONIUS. Have you seen Cossatius's play?

SEVERUS. Yes, it's clever, but——

HYGERIUS. That kind of play ought not to be tolerated. It undermines the principles of morality.

SEVERUS. Morals have nothing to do with art.

HYGERIUS. I repeat that these kinds of plays are the ruin of the Empire.

PETRONIUS. I see you are on the side of the " Extensionists."

HYGERIUS. I don't know what you mean by an " Extensionist," but if you mean a Roman and a patriot——

PETRONIUS. No, I mean a Greek and a swindler.

PROTEUS. Excellent eels—try them.

RUFUS. Let me beg you not to touch them; they are full of poison.

DEMOPHILUS (*alarmed*). Poison ! Who's poisoned them ?

PETRONIUS. Rufus means they give you gout.

PROTEUS. I once knew a man who ate twenty-seven eels for a bet.

DEMOPHILUS (*really interested*). Oh ! Did he win ?

PROTEUS. Yes; but he died afterwards. Hush ! the speeches are beginning.

PETRONIUS. Oh dear ! Oh dear !

[*The* PREFECT OF PUTEOLI *rises farther up the table.*

THE PREFECT. Friends and citizens, and more especially, citizens of Puteoli and Baiæ : It is with feelings of peculiar emotion that I rise to propose that toast, which of all toasts is the nearest to the heart and leaps most readily to the lips of a Roman —I mean, of course, the toast of our beloved Emperor. I may say that in all the vast extent of this Empire, of which we are so justly proud, the Emperor has no more loyal subjects than those of Baiæ and—(*cheers*)—of Puteoli. (*Cheers.*) Although in the past we of Puteoli may not always have been able to see eye to eye with our neighbours of Baiæ, in matters of local administration, to-day, happily, all such rivalry has ended. And to whom is this due? To whom but the Emperor, who, with his knowledge of the Roman heart, has had the happy, the graceful, nay, more, the truly Imperial and the truly Roman idea of joining the two cities by this elegant and monumental bridge. (*Loud cheers.*) We of Puteoli are not quick to forget the benefits we have received in the past from the Imperial Family. And some of us who are here present remember that auspicious and never-to-be-forgotten day when the Emperor's illustrious father, the ever-memorable Germanicus—(*loud and prolonged cheers*)—I say many of us here present will recall that thrice-memorable occasion when the illustrious Germanicus—(*loud cheers*)—paid us a visit. Romans, I have no wish to rake up things which are better forgotten; I have no desire to abuse the ashes of him who, whatever his faults and his failings may have been, is now for ever beyond the reach of our recrimination. We Romans have a proverb which says : " Of the dead nothing but good "—(*cheers*)—and you, citizens of Puteoli and Baiæ, have ever strictly observed, both by precept and by practice, the wisdom that has been handed down to us in the popular phrases of the Roman people. (*Cheers.*) Therefore, it is with no fear of being misunderstood, and in no carping or unjust spirit, that I say that the example which our beloved Emperor Caligula is daily setting us, both in peace and in war, and in all the arts and graces of life—this example is, I say, as it were, heightened when we—and we of Puteoli and Baiæ are especially sensible of the fact—when we think of the short-comings and the mistakes of the late and unfortunate Tiberius—(*hisses and groans*)—shortcomings and mistakes to which our present Emperor out so swift

an end, and out of whose ashes he bade our Empire
and our Government, our internal affairs and our
foreign policy, rise rejuvenated and splendid like
the Phœnix. (*Cheers.*) Citizens, I will detain you
no longer. All I will say is this : so long as we have
at the head of us one who is the pattern of what a
Roman gentleman should be, one who is at the same
time the elder brother and the father of his people,
so long as this shall be, so long will the Roman
Empire, throughout all its length and breadth, act
together in that same spirit of fraternal love and unity,
bound by ties as strong as that with which our
Emperor has to-day united and linked the people of
Baiæ to the people of Puteoli. Citizens, I propose
the health of the divine Emperor. (*Loud cheers.
The toast is drunk with enthusiasm.*)

HYGERIUS. A first-rate speech.

THE PREFECT OF BAIÆ *rises*. Citizens, it is with
the keenest sense of my unfitness to so exalted a task
that I rise to propose the toast which is second on
our list, that toast which of all others, with the exception of that which we have just drunk, is most
grateful to Roman ears, namely, the Army. (*Cheers.*)
Although not a soldier myself, my heart is with the
Army; but I will go farther, I will say that all of us,
whatever our avocations may be, whether we be
lawyers, merchants, engineers, painters, poets, philo-
sophers, are in a sense soldiers of the Emperor.
(*Cheers.*) And Peace, citizens, has its battles as well
as War. (*Loud Cheers.*) To-day we are gathered
together to celebrate one of those battles—a battle
which has ended in a triumph. (*Cheers.*) [DEMO-
PHILUS (*aside*). What battle?] I allude to the
completion of this handsome bridge—(*cheers*)—

which is a notable—I may even say an unparalleled example—of the triumph of man's will over the elements. As the immortal poet Camerinus—(*cheers*) —has said :

O'er vanquished Nature Man shall spread his sway,
And force the fretful ocean to obey

(*Cheers.*)

And while the utmost credit is due to the skill and patience with which the engineers, Demonax and Hegias, of Corinth, have executed their stupendous task, still greater praise is due to the Emperor, in whose fertile brain the great idea had its origin, and without whose unceasing aid and constant interest it could never have been completed. (*Cheers.*) We of Baiæ know how keen was that interest, how valuable that aid, and we will never forget it. I have said, citizens, we are all of us in a sense soldiers, and it is a sight like this, an occasion such as to-day's, that brings home to every Roman the self-sacrifice, the patience, the stubborn will, and the dogged persistence—qualities all of them essentially military —of the Roman race. I therefore propose the health of the Army, coupled with the name of its glorious Commander-in-Chief, the Emperor. (*Loud cheers. The toast is drunk.*)

SEVERUS. He misquoted Camerinus.

[*A* PRÆTORIAN OFFICER *rises.*

THE PRÆTORIAN OFFICER. Citizens, my trade is to speak and not to act—I mean to act and not to speak. (*Loud cheers.*) I am a humble particle of what has so rightly been called the great dumb one. (*Cheers.*) I thank you all very much for drinking the last toast, and I in my turn have great pleasure in proposing the toast which comes next on the list, namely, the toast of Literature. (*Cheers.*) I am not much of a literary man myself, but I greatly enjoy reading the description of battles in the works of that poet who, though not a Roman by birth, is practically a Roman—I mean Homer—(*cheers*)—and also in the great epic of our Roman Homer, I mean Camerinus. (*Loud cheers.*) I propose the toast of Literature, coupled with that of the divine Emperor, who, as we all know, is a first-rate author himself. (*Cheers.*)

[EROTIANUS, *an elderly poet, rises to reply.*

EROTIANUS. Citizens, great and immortal names have been mentioned to-day. Homer, Camerinus, have lent by the very mention of their names a diviner light to this already illustrious occasion. Nor has our gallant friend in his masterly oration failed to remind us of the talents, the brilliant and exceptional literary gifts, of our noble master. (*Cheers.*) I am the last person who should address you on this theme. (*Cries of No, No.*) We had hoped that Seneca—(*cheers*)—whose verses are for ever on our lips, would be present. Unfortunately a bad cold has detained him in Rome. Æsculapius has conquered the Muses —(*cries of Shame*)—and instead of a brilliant literary light you have the flicker of a new artisan in the field of letters. (*Cries of No, No.*) I am, if I may say so, no more than a humble shepherd on the slopes of Parnassus. But, citizens, those slopes are so high, and so wide that there is room on them for the greatest, such as Homer and Ovid—(*cheers*)—and for the more humble but none the less painstaking, such as Virgil and myself. (*Cheers.*) I will now proceed to read

to you a short epic in six cantos which I have pre-
pared for this occasion. (*Cheers. He clears his
throat.*) It is called " The Bridge." (*Cheers.*)

> ⌐*The* EMPEROR *makes a signal, upon which a regi-
> ment of Prætorians, concealed in a neighbouring
> tent, rush among the guests armed with swords
> and sharp tridents, and proceed to toss them
> into the sea. The meal breaks up in confusion.
> Some of the guests escape, but a large number
> are drowned, including* EROTIANUS.

CURTAIN.

XI

THE AULIS DIFFICULTY

SCENE.—AGAMEMNON'S *tent at Aulis. Discovered:* AGAMEMNON *seated at a camp table writing.*

Enter IPHIGENIA

IPHIGENIA. Do you want to speak to me, papa?

AGAMEMNON (*nervously*). Yes, yes, a moment. (*A pause.*)

IPHIGENIA. Well?

AGAMEMNON. Sit down—on that chair—it's more comfortable there. . . . I . . . er . . . (*A pause.*)

IPHIGENIA. If you've got nothing particular to say, papa, I'll go, if you don't mind; because mamma wants me to help her with the dinner. The cook is quite helpless——

AGAMEMNON. Wait a minute. I do want to speak to you very particularly. . . . (*A pause.*) . . . It's a lovely day again to-day.

IPHIGENIA. Really, papa——

AGAMEMNON. It's not so irrelevant as you think. You see, there's not a breath of wind.

IPHIGENIA. I know. They say it's quite impossible for you to start.

AGAMEMNON. We shall have been here two months next Tuesday.

IPHIGENIA. You mean next Saturday.

AGAMEMNON. Tuesday or Saturday, it's all the same.

IPHIGENIA. It's a mercy we did stop here. Mamma says that your linen was in a dreadful state, and that if she hadn't come out she doesn't know how you would have managed.

AGAMEMNON. Yes, I don't say that the stay hasn't been of some use; but now it is absolutely essential that we should get to Troy.

IPHIGENIA. Why don't you start to-day?

AGAMEMNON. Whenever we put to sea there's either no wind at all, or a gale which drives us straight back home.

IPHIGENIA. It is very tiresome, but it can't be helped, can it?

AGAMEMNON. Well, that's just it. I'm afraid it can be helped.

IPHIGENIA. What do you mean, papa?

AGAMEMNON. To cut a long story short, Calchas consulted the Oracle this morning, and it appears, he says, I mean the Oracle said, or rather the goddess——

IPHIGENIA. Which goddess?

AGAMEMNON. Artemis.

IPHIGENIA. Oh, she's impossible.

AGAMEMNON. Well, as I told you, Calchas says that it is Artemis who is causing the delay by sending us adverse winds, and——

IPHIGENIA. Can't something be done?

AGAMEMNON. That is precisely the point. The goddess has, through the Oracle, suggested a way out of the difficulty, and it concerns you.

IPHIGENIA. Me? What can I have to do with it?

AGAMEMNON. Now, my dearest Iphigenia, I want you to be reasonable. You always were a sensible girl, and I want to you bring all your good sense to bear on this . . . in this . . . er . . . trying occasion.

IPHIGENIA. I don't understand.

AGAMEMNON. I will go straight to the point. Artemis says that we shall never leave Aulis unless you consent to go through the form of being sacrificed to her.

IPHIGENIA. What do you mean by " going through the form " ?

AGAMEMNON. I mean that in all probability . . . in fact, quite certainly, the sacrifice would be purely a formal one, and that there is every chance . . . in fact, I may say it is almost certain that one of the other gods or goddesses would intervene at the last moment and prevent the sacrifice from being fatal.

IPHIGENIA. You mean to say that there is not the slightest chance of my being killed—that it's only a farce?

AGAMEMNON. I won't go so far as that . . . but I will say that as far as we know every precedent in the past——

IPHIGENIA. Oh, bother the precedents. What I want to know is this: Is there the slightest chance of my being *really* sacrificed?

AGAMEMNON. It is highly improbable, of course; only you *must* consent; you must behave exactly as if you were going to be sacrificed; you must express your entire willingness to lay down your life for your country; and knowing what a patriotic, obedient, filial child you are, I am certain this will be a positive pleasure to you.

IPHIGENIA. I won't.

AGAMEMNON. You mean you won't even pretend to——

IPHIGENIA. I won't have anything to do with it at all—I think it's monstrous, and I'm sure mamma will agree with me.

AGAMEMNON. My dearest child, let me beg of you not to say a word about this to your mother just yet.

IPHIGENIA. Of course, I shall tell her. (*Enter* CLYTÆMNESTRA.) Here is mamma. Mamma——

CLYTÆMNESTRA. What is all this?

IPHIGENIA. Papa says I must be sacrificed to Artemis, in order that they may have a smooth passage to Troy, and to prevent Ajax being sea-sick. I say I won't. (*She begins to cry.*)

CLYTÆMNESTRA (*taking her in her arms*). Of course you shan't, my love—my darling. (*To* AGAMEMNON) What is this ridiculous nonsense?

AGAMEMNON. I assure you it is not my doing. I merely repeated what Calchas had said. He consulted the Oracle, and it appears that Artemis is vexed : she is, in fact, very much displeased. She says we shall never leave Aulis unless Iphigenia consents to go through the form of being sacrificed— of course it's only a matter of form—but she must consent.

CLYTÆMNESTRA. I see. As long as I'm here my child shall not degrade herself by being a party to any ridiculous farce of this nature. I don't care a bit if we do stay here. You ought never to have come here for one thing. I always said it was absurd from the first—just because of Helen's silly escapade. If you can't get a fair wind you'll have to go home ; but you shan't touch Iphigenia.

Enter a MAID

THE MAID (*to* CLYTÆMNESTRA). The cook wants to know whether the fish are to be boiled or fried.

CLYTÆMNESTRA (*angrily*). I told her fried. (*To* AGAMEMNON) I must go and look after her. I'll be back in a moment.

[*Exit* CLYTÆMNESTRA.

AGAMEMNON. There, you see what you've done. You've set your mother against the whole plan.

IPHIGENIA (*crying*). I hope I have. Of course, if you want to kill me, please do . . . just (*sobbing*) as if I were a sheep.

AGAMEMNON. My dear child, do be calm. Who ever talked of killing——

Enter CALCHAS

AGAMEMNON. She won't hear of it.

CALCHAS. My dear child, please be sensible and think of the interests at stake. Remember you are grown up, and we grown-up people have to face these things.

IPHIGENIA. I don't care what you say, I won't be sacrificed—I won't be killed like a sheep.

CALCHAS. Even if the worst came to the worst, I promise you you would feel no pain. I assure you we have reached a pitch of perfection in the working of these things which makes all accidents impossible. Besides, think of the honour and the glory.

AGAMEMNON. And it's not as if she would be killed *really*.

CALCHAS. It's extremely improbable; but even

if she were to lose consciousness and not recover, I am sure most girls would envy her. Just think, your statue would be put up in every city in Greece.

AGAMEMNON. All the poets would celebrate her.

CALCHAS. You see it's not as if she were married.

AGAMEMNON. She has always refused every one.

CALCHAS. And now it's too late.

AGAMEMNON. Girls are so independent nowadays.

CALCHAS. They think nothing of tradition, country, or of the respect they owe their parents. They are ungrateful.

AGAMEMNON. They never think of what they owe the goddesses. In my time . . .

Enter ODYSSEUS

IPHIGENIA. I don't care what you say. I won't be sacrificed. (*She bursts into tears.*)

[ODYSSEUS *whispers to* AGAMEMNON *and* CALCHAS *to withdraw. They go out.*

ODYSSEUS. And how is our little Iphigenia today?

IPHIGENIA (*drying her eyes*). Quite well, thank you; only papa wants to kill me.

ODYSSEUS. Kill you, my dear child! I assure you you are mistaken. Nobody, and least of all your father, could dream of such a thing. You are the life and soul of the expedition. It was only this morning I wrote to Penelope to tell her how well you were looking and what a difference it made to all of us your being here.

IPHIGENIA. Papa wants me to be sacrificed.

ODYSSEUS. You can't have understood your father. Let me explain it to you. You know what Artemis is: she's a charming goddess—quite charming—only she's touchy. Well, she happens to be very much put out at this moment by the attention that has been paid to the other goddesses; and by a very regrettable oversight her sacrifice has been neglected once or twice lately. Of course she is put out; but, believe me, the situation only requires tact—just a little tact . . . and we all want you to help us. . . . You see, if you don't help us we are lost, and the whole expedition may be ruined, all just for the want of a little tact at the right moment. Now, nobody can help us as well as you can. You see Artemis has taken a peculiar fancy to you. She admires you enormously. I happen to know this on the very best authority. She thinks you are far more beautiful than your Aunt Helen. At the same time she is just a shade hurt that you never take any notice of her. Now, what we want you to do is to consent to our stratagem: a delicate piece of flattery which will soothe Artemis and make everything all right. All you will have to do is to wear the most beautiful dress—white and silver—and a band of wrought gold studded with rubies round your head, and to walk with your wonderful hair reaching almost to your feet, in a procession of weeping maidens to the Temple; and there, after the usual prayers and chants, you will sing a hymn to Artemis, especially composed for the occasion, to a flute accompaniment; then, in the gaze of all the crowd, you will kneel down before the altar, and Artemis, flattered and pleased, will carry you off in a cloud, and substitute a sheep or something else for you. Every one will praise you; you will have had all the amusement of the festival, all the glory and honour of the sacrifice, and none of the inconvenience.

IPHIGENIA (*pensively*). It would be rather fun. Are you sure I shouldn't risk being killed really? Calchas said I probably would.

ODYSSEUS. Calchas knows nothing about it at all. I promise you that it's just as safe as if you were going to sing at the festival of Bacchus.

IPHIGENIA. But what will happen to me afterwards?

ODYSSEUS. That must be a secret between you and me. Artemis has arranged that a charming young man shall carry you away. I need not mention his name, as you know it too well. It begins with an A. But the marriage must remain a secret until after the siege.

IPHIGENIA. All right, I will do it. I mean I will pretend to consent, but there must be no question of its really coming off. That you must swear.

ODYSSEUS. I swear we shall sacrifice a sheep instead of you, or if the worst comes to the worst Achilles' slave, who is so like you.

IPHIGENIA. And then I shall really marry Achilles.

Enter CLYTÆMNESTRA

ODYSSEUS (*to* CLYTÆMNESTRA). It's all settled; only don't discuss it with Agamemnon. He doesn't quite know how to deal with goddesses. He is—you forgive me saying so—a little bit heavy.

CLYTÆMNESTRA (*to* IPHIGENIA). You don't mean to say you've consented. I forbid it. . . . I am your mother, and I positively forbid you to do any such thing.

IPHIGENIA. I'm of age. I'm old enough to judge what I can do and what I can't do. It's my duty, and it's a question of principle; and if I choose to be sacrificed, nobody has the right to prevent me. And I *do* choose. The one thing I've always longed for all my life has been to die for my country.

[*Exit* IPHIGENIA *in a passion.*

[ODYSSEUS *looks at* CLYTÆMNESTRA *and smiles.*

CLYTÆMNESTRA. Serpent!

CURTAIN.

XII

DON JUAN'S FAILURE

SCENE.—*The hall in an English Country House.
Van Dyck Period.*

LUCASTA. My mother will be down directly, if
you don't mind waiting.

DON JUAN. On the contrary, I could wait a hundred
years in the company of one whom I know not whether
she be a goddess or a mortal.

LUCASTA (*blushing*). It's very kind of you to say
so, sir, but I am very busy this morning. I am wanted
at the farm to see about the cows.

DON JUAN. Fortunate cows! But cannot they
wait a moment? Surely there is no desperate hurry?

LUCASTA. I am late already, sir, and I am loath
to keep people waiting.

DON JUAN. How nice, how considerate and charming of you. I adore those who are loath to keep others
waiting. It is the revelation of a delightful nature.
I am sure we shall be friends. I feel as if we had
always known one another.

LUCASTA. Oh, sir, but I do not even know your
name! I only know you are the Spanish nobleman
who was expected.

DON JUAN (*proudly*). My name is one you may
perhaps have heard of. I am Don Juan of Seville.

LUCASTA. One of our ponies is called Don Juan—the old one. It takes the children out in a cart : but he's lame now.

DON JUAN (*vexed*). You must let me give you a horse, a fiery steed fit to carry you, for I'm sure you ride like Diana, and you shall call that Don Juan.

LUCASTA. Thank you, sir, but my mother says one must never accept gifts from strangers.

DON JUAN. But I am not a stranger. You must not look upon me as a stranger. You must look upon me as a friend.

LUCASTA. Mistress Markham says that one has no right to call people friends until one has known them for seven years.

DON JUAN. Who is Mistress Markham?

LUCASTA. She is our governess.

DON JUAN. She knows nothing about it. Believe me, all governesses are fools.

LUCASTA. Not Mistress Markham. She knows everything—even the Greek irregular verbs.

DON JUAN. Well, let us admit, then, that there is only one thing she doesn't know.

LUCASTA. What, sir?

DON JUAN. The birth, the growth, and the nature of our friendship. May not I claim to be a friend? You surely do not wish to regard me as an enemy?

LUCASTA (*after reflecting*). Well, I suppose there's no harm; because I do not suppose it is wrong to make friends with old people.

DON JUAN (*laughing uneasily*). I am old enough to claim friendship with you; but I am not so old as all that. Do I look so very old?

LUCASTA (*blushing*). Oh no, sir. I never meant that, I'm sure. All I meant was that you were old compared with my friends.

DON JUAN. Have you many friends?

LUCASTA. Oh yes! There's Harry, who has just left school; and Philip, he is a student at Oxford; and Valentine, he is about to join the Yeomanry; and my cousin Dick, he is my greatest friend.

DON JUAN. How old is he?

LUCASTA. He left school six months ago. He's going to be a great soldier, like Sir Philip Sidney.

DON JUAN. Oh! and are you very fond of him?

LUCASTA. Very. He plays tennis better than any one. Do you play tennis, sir?

DON JUAN. I'm afraid I don't.

LUCASTA. Bowls?

DON JUAN. I'm afraid not either.

LUCASTA. Rounders?

DON JUAN. I'm afraid I don't play any games except draughts and lansquenet.

LUCASTA. Lansquenet and draughts are indoor games. We don't count them. Cousin Dick says they are all very well for women.

DON JUAN. You see, I never have time for that kind of thing.

LUCASTA. Are you an officer, sir?

DON JUAN. Oh no!

LUCASTA. A sailor?

DON JUAN. No; I hate the sea.

LUCASTA. I suppose you are a discoverer. Spaniards are such great travellers.

DON JUAN. No; I have only travelled in Europe and for pleasure.

LUCASTA. How stupid of me, sir. You are, of course, a diplomatist.

DON JUAN. No: I am merely a gentleman at large.

LUCASTA. Do you mean you follow no profession?

DON JUAN. No profession exactly, but many occupations.

LUCASTA. But how do you contrive to pass the time?

DON JUAN. Well, you see, we Spaniards are different from you English. We are less practical, and more—what shall I say?—more fiery, more impatient, more romantic. We consider it quite enough for a man who is a Spaniard and a nobleman as I am, nay, more, we consider that such a man can have no nobler occupation than to devote his life, his heart, his brain to the constant and daily service and worship of a beautiful woman.

LUCASTA. Oh, I see; you are engaged to be married.

DON JUAN. No, alas!

LUCASTA. Haven't you got enough money to marry on?

DON JUAN. It's not that: my purse is equal to my station.

LUCASTA. Her parents, I suppose, have refused their consent.

DON JUAN. I have not yet asked them.

LUCASTA. I wish you all success, sir.

DON JUAN. But you don't understand, most charming and gracious of Englishwomen. It is true that I love. I am consumed with a love which will never diminish nor die, a love that burns within me like a raging fever; but I have not yet dared to speak it. The divine and adorable creature whom I worship does not suspect the cruel plight I am in. She ignores my flame.

LUCASTA. Why do you not tell her, sir?

DON JUAN. Ah! That is so easily said! But what if she were to take offence? What if I were by a too sudden and abrupt declaration of the passion that consumes me to nip in the bud all chance of my love finding a response in her breast? What if I by a too hasty word were to shatter my hopes for ever?

LUCASTA. Is she so very young? Pardon me, sir, if I am wrong in asking.

DON JUAN. You could never do wrong. No fault could ever mar those faultless lips. (LUCASTA *blushes.*) I will tell you she is very young, and I have only seen her once.

LUCASTA. Then it was a case of love at first sight?

DON JUAN. Yes, but love is a weak word to express the great wave which has carried me away.

LUCASTA. They say that love at first sight is often mutual.

DON JUAN. I pray Heaven that it may be so in this case; but I doubt if she has guessed my sweet and bitter secret. She is so young, so innocent.

LUCASTA. Is she fair or dark, sir?

DON JUAN. Her hair is the colour of your hair, and, like yours, it has the glitter of sunshine, with miraculous shades and adorable crisping curls like those that wreathe your brow. Her skin is like yours; that is to say, a rose lately sprinkled with dew. Her eyes are the colour of your eyes; that is to say, they have the radiance of the azure sky and depth of the summer sea. Her nose is the pictured semblance of your nose, delicate as a flower, tip-tilted, transparent, enchanting. Her lips are like your lips; they put to shame ripe cherries, red roses, and rubies; and her teeth are like your teeth, more perfect than Orient pearls. She has your carriage, your grace and rhythm of movement, the stately poise of your head, and the divine contour of your form. She has the radiance of your smile and the laughing music of your speech.

LUCASTA. It is very kind of you, sir, to compare me to so well-favoured a person.

DON JUAN. I am not comparing you to her. I am comparing her to you. Until this morning I did not know that such beauty could live and breathe.

LUCASTA. Did you see her this morning for the first time?

DON JUAN. Yes, it was this morning; to-day is the fatal day that has changed the earth for me to a giddy ladder suspended between heaven and hell.

LUCASTA. Then I know who it is. It is Electra Harrington our neighbour. You saw her on your way here.

DON JUAN. Believe me, it was no Electra Harrington. Electra Harrington would be a wrinkled hag in comparison with the goddess whom I worship. But tell me, do you think I might dare to plead my cause? Do you think there is the frailest hope of her listening to my suit?

LUCASTA. Why not? I am sure, sir, any girl would feel very much flattered at the attentions of a nobleman such as yourself.

DON JUAN. But you said I was old.

LUCASTA. Oh, sir, I told you I never meant that.

All I meant was that you were grown-up and a man, and not a schoolboy like Philip.

Don Juan. Then you think that a maiden could look at me without disgust?

Lucasta. Oh, sir!

Don Juan. Even if at first I found her heart hard as adamant, if she will only let me plead my cause I feel certain I can soften it. That is all I ask—a hearing.

Lucasta. I should tell her at once, sir, in your place. Girls are often bashful. (*She blushes.*)

Don Juan. Then there is another grisly fear that haunts me. She may already have given her heart away. She may already have a betrothed.

Lucasta. That is not likely if it's any of the girls in our county. They are all so young; and the others are married—except Dianeme, and then she's a fright, so it could hardly be her.

Don Juan. Then you think I ought to be bold?

Lucasta (*clapping her hands*). Oh yes, do be bold!

[Don Juan *seizes* Lucasta *and endeavours to kiss her. She gives him a very smart box on the ears.*

Lucasta. Sir, what does this unpardonable liberty mean? I thought you were a gentleman and a nobleman.

Don Juan (*kneeling*). Forgive me. I thought you had understood. I thought you must have guessed —don't interrupt me, only hear me—I thought you must have known when I described to you my heart's desire; when I told you that you had her every feature; but I was mad. It was unpardonable of me; but hear me all the same, Lucasta; adorable, lovely, perfect Lucasta, I love you; I love you passionately. I offer you my hand, my life, my fortune.

LUCASTA. Please get up, sir. I hate men who kneel—they look so silly; and if you are going to talk nonsense any more I shall go upstairs.

DON JUAN (*rising*). Then you mean that I may not even hope?

LUCASTA (*bursting into peals of laughter*). Forgive me, but I can't help it.

DON JUAN. It is really no laughing matter. (*He draws his sword.*) I am ready to stab myself.

LUCASTA (*still shaking with laughter*). Please do not be so foolish. Why, you're much older than my father. Here is my mother.

Enter the COUNTESS OF WESSEX, *a handsome lady. She curtsies deeply.*

LUCASTA (*aside to her mother*). Oh! he's so funny.

　　[*She runs away, vainly suppressing a peal of laughter.*

CURTAIN.

XIII

CALPURNIA'S DINNER-PARTY

SCENE.—*A room in* JULIUS CÆSAR'S *house. Discovered :* JULIUS CÆSAR *and* CALPURNIA.

CALPURNIA. Catullus has accepted, so that will make us thirteen.

CÆSAR. I won't sit down thirteen to dinner; it isn't fair to one's guests.

CALPURNIA. What nonsense ! They none of them mind.

CÆSAR. I beg your pardon. I happen to know that Cicero is intensely superstitious. Of course I don't mind personally, but one must think of others.

CALPURNIA. Then what shall we do?

CÆSAR. Ask some one else.

CALPURNIA. Then you must get another man. You are sure to see some one at the Forum.

CÆSAR. I will ask Calvus.

CALPURNIA. How like a man. In the first place he is in mourning.

CÆSAR. Who for?

CALPURNIA. Quintilla, of course.

CÆSAR. We need not go into that.

CALPURNIA. He won't go anywhere—at present —but even if it wasn't for that, don't you see that it would quite spoil the dinner to ask Calvus with Catullus?

CÆSAR.   Why?

CALPURNIA.   Because they both write poetry.

CÆSAR.   What does that matter?

CALPURNIA.   Of course, if you want to spoil the dinner——

CÆSAR.   Must it be a man?

CALPURNIA.   Yes; we have got quite enough women.

CÆSAR.   Why not ask Atticus?

CALPURNIA.   Then we should have to ask Pilia.

CÆSAR.   She hates going out.

CALPURNIA.   It is impossible to ask him without her—and I won't ask her; she would ruin the dinner. Besides, I told you we can't have another woman.

CÆSAR.   What about Cinna?

CALPURNIA.   Cornelia's got him.   She always gives a dinner the same night as I do, so as to take away the people I want from me.

CÆSAR.   I can't think of anybody.

CALPURNIA.   You will see some one at the Forum; but mind you are careful, and don't ask some one nobody else knows, or some one whom they all hate.

CÆSAR.   There's nobody in Rome just now.

Enter a SLAVE, *with a letter for* CALPURNIA

THE SLAVE.   They are waiting for a verbal answer.
          [CALPURNIA *takes the letter and reads it.*

CALPURNIA.   It is from Lucullus; he wants us to dine with him to night—quite a tiny dinner, he says—he wants us to taste some oysters from Britain.

CÆSAR.   I suppose we can't put off our guests?

CALPURNIA.   Certainly not.   It *is* unlucky. (*She sits down at a table and writes an answer.*)   It is the sort of thing that's sure to happen.   I wish you hadn't asked all these people.

CÆSAR.   I didn't ask a soul.

CALPURNIA (*to the* SLAVE).   There's the answer.

The SLAVE *bows and retires.   He returns again immediately with another letter, which he gives to* CALPURNIA.

CALPURNIA.   Is there an answer?

THE SLAVE.   The slave is waiting.

CALPURNIA (*reading out*).   " MOST ILLUSTRIOUS AND CELESTIALLY FAVOURED CALPURNIA "—it is from the Persian Ambassador—" Pity me.   The gods are most cruel and unpropitious.   Owing to the extraordinary carelessness of my private secretary I find that I have been engaged for several weeks to dine with Lucullus to-night.   As I only know him slightly, I am sure you will understand that in this case I must sacrifice pleasure to duty, and miss a brilliant and charming evening.   Alas, alas, pity me!—Your slave, ZOROASTER SORHAB JEMSHID." (*To the* SLAVE) Say I quite understand.   (*Exit* SLAVE.)   Jemshid always, always throws one over.

Enter the SLAVE *with two letters.   He gives one to* CÆSAR *and one to* CALPURNIA

THE SLAVE.   Both waiting for an answer.

CALPURNIA.   Who is yours from?

CÆSAR.   Mark Antony.   (*He reads*) " DEAR OLD BOY—I am frightfully sorry, but I can't dine with you to-night.   I have had a tooth pulled out this morning, and the doctor says I mustn't go out, worse luck.   My respects to Calpurnia.   I will look in to-morrow if I am well enough.   Don't bother to come and see me, as I can't talk.—M.A."

CALPURNIA. He's dining with Lucullus, of course. If you had only let me engage that cook from Gaul, nobody would ever throw us over.

CÆSAR. Who is yours from?

CALPURNIA. Lucilius. (*She reads*) " MOST ILLUSTRIOUS AND EXQUISITE CALPURNIA—I have got into the most frightful muddle. Last Monday, Lucullus asked me to dinner to-night, and I accepted. Then the next day I wrote to him and said I could not dine with him after all, as I had to go into Court the day after, and I should have to work all night. The day after I wrote this letter my case was put off, and then you kindly asked me to dinner, and of course I accepted; and now Lucullus has found out that I am dining with you, and thinks I threw him over for you. He says he's a man short, and that as I was engaged to him first, I simply must come to his dinner. So I am writing to know whether you could possibly let me off? And, as I have already been obliged to throw Lucullus over twice lately, I am sure you will understand that I cannot very well come to you to-night. I am too sorry for words.— LUCILIUS."

CÆSAR. I suppose the answer is " Very well " in both cases.

CALPURNIA. Yes. (*Exit* SLAVE.) Of course they will all throw us over now.

CÆSAR. Well, in that case, the matter would be solved, and we could dine with Lucullus.

CALPURNIA. But they won't *all* throw us over. Portia's certain to come.

Enter the SLAVE *with two letters.   He gives them to* CALPURNIA

THE SLAVE. No answer.

CALPURNIA (*eagerly*). This is from Clodia. I wonder what lie she will tell. (*Reads*) " DARLING CALPURNIA—I am *too, too* miserable. Everything has gone stupidly wrong. When you asked me to dinner and said Friday, I thought Friday was the 10th, and now I see it is the 11th, and I have been engaged for ages to that tiresome old Lucullus. Of course I would throw him over *at once*, but Metellus won't hear of it, and he says it will serve me right if you never ask us again. So like a husband ! It is *too* unlucky, darling, isn't it ? You will feel for me, I am sure.—Your loving CLODIA." Well, Catullus won't come now.

CÆSAR. Is the other letter from him ?

CALPURNIA. No. Of course they wouldn't send them together. It is from Cicero ; if he can't come, our dinner's ruined. (*She reads*) " MOST HONOURED AND EXCELLENT CALPURNIA—Owing to a quite unusual press of business I much regret to say that I shall be compelled to forgo the pleasure of enjoying your kind hospitality to-night. The misfortune is all the more heavy since I shall not only miss the pleasure of enjoying your charming society, but also the opportunity of discussing several matters of importance with Cæsar, which I was particularly anxious to do. Believe me, I am consumed with regret, but I will not waste your time in vain excuses and apologies, which seem only to increase my vexation without diminishing the inconvenience I fear I may be causing you. Hail and farewell.—M. T. CICERO."

Enter the SLAVE *with a letter for* CÆSAR

THE SLAVE. No answer. (*He goes out.*)

CÆSAR (*opening the letter*). It is from Catullus. (*Reading*) " A terrible catastrophe has happened. Going home last night from the Esquiline I got my feet wet, and this has affected my style; my hexameters are beginning to limp and my elegiacs are gouty. The doctor says the only thing which can cure me is a quiet night's rest and some, oysters from Britain. But it is unlikely that I shall find any in Rome. In view of these distressing circumstances I fear I must put off coming to-night to your dinnerparty. Quite seriously, I am unwell. With a thousand compliments to Calpurnia.—Wretched CATULLUS." " *P.S.*—I was half engaged to Lucullus to-night, so if you see him later, tell him I *was* going to dine with you."

CALPURNIA. How silly he is ! I shall never ask him again.

CÆSAR. Who is there left?

CALPURNIA. Now, there are only Brutus and Portia, Cassius and Cynthia.

Enter the SLAVE *with a letter for* CALPURNIA.
She takes it.

THE SLAVE. No answer. (*He goes out.*)

CALPURNIA. It is from Cynthia. I thought she would throw us over too. (*Reads*) " DEAREST CALPURNIA—Lucullus says you and Cæsar and Catullus and Clodia are all dining with him. Is that right? Am I dining with him or with you? Please arrange it with him. I will do exactly what you like.—Your loving CYNTHIA." Now we have only got the bores left, Cassius, Brutus and Portia. I don't suppose we can very well put them off.

CÆSAR. I think we might in this case. You see,

it is perfectly true that our guests have all thrown us over, and it is much too late now to get any one else.

CALPURNIA. Very well. You must write to Cassius and I will write to Portia.

CÆSAR. And then we can dine with Lucullus.

CALPURNIA. Just as you think best; but if Brutus and Portia find it out they will never forgive us.

CÆSAR. What nonsense! Besides, perhaps Lucullus will ask them.

CALPURNIA. Never. (*Reading out as she writes*) DEAREST PORTIA—It is too unlucky, we are obliged to put off our dinner-party after all, because everybody has thrown us over; we are dreadfully disappointed, as we had so looked forward to seeing you. We shall have our little dinner on the 19th instead —Friday week. We do so hope you and Brutus are free.—Yours, Calpurnia.

CÆSAR. That's all right. I will write to Lucullus and say we will come, if he has still got room for us.

CALPURNIA. Just as you like; but remember that Brutus is touchy and that Portia never forgives.

CURTAIN.

XIV

LUCULLUS'S DINNER-PARTY

SCENE.—*A room in* LUCULLUS's *house. Discovered:* LUCULLUS (*an old man*) *and his* COOK.

LUCULLUS. Of course, I don't say that it wasn't a good dish; but it was not Neapolitan peacock.

THE COOK. They were straight from Naples; the same as we've always had, sir.

LUCULLUS (*irritated*). I'm not talking about the bird, but about the dish. You know as well as I do that Neapolitan peacock without anemone seed is not Neapolitan peacock. And then the nightingales' tongues were over-roasted. They ought to be roasted for twenty-three minutes and not one second longer.

THE COOK. They were only twenty-four minutes on the roast.

LUCULLUS. There, you see, it was that extra minute that spoilt them. You might just as well not roast them at all as roast them for twenty-four minutes. And then there were too many butterflies' wings round the sturgeon.

THE COOK. The chief slave——

LUCULLUS. I've told you over and over again, till I'm tired of saying it, that the chief slave has nothing to do with the arrangement of the dishes.

That is your affair. The chief slave can arrange the table, but he must not touch the dishes. The look of a dish is just as important as the taste of it. And then there was a pinch too much salt in the wild boar sauce.

THE COOK. The first sauceman has just lost his wife.

LUCULLUS. That's not my affair. Please make it clear that this must not happen again. The fact is, Æmilius, you're falling off—last night's dinner wasn't fit to eat; it was filthy; the kind of food one gets at Cæsar's—sent for from round the corner.

THE COOK. If I may be so bold as to say so, we were saying in the kitchen that these rehearsals of dinners the night before the real dinner make us nervous——

LUCULLUS. All I can say is, if you can't cook a good dinner twice running you'd better get another place. The dinner wasn't fit to eat, and if it's anything like that to-night I advise you to give up trying to cook and to take to wrestling. That's all; you can go.

[*The* COOK *blushes scarlet and goes out.*

Enter a SLAVE

THE SLAVE. Can you see Portia, the wife of Brutus?

LUCULLUS. Yes; show her in.

Enter PORTIA

PORTIA. It's such a beautiful morning that I thought a nice brisk walk would do me good, and as I was passing your door I couldn't help just looking in.

LUCULLUS. I'm delighted.

PORTIA (*sitting down*). I wanted to ask you whether you would mind giving your patronage to the Old Slaves' Pensions Fund? Cicero has helped us a great deal, and Cæsar has promised. By the way, is Cæsar dining with you to-night?

LUCULLUS. Yes, I believe he is.

PORTIA. Well, he particularly wants to see Brutus, and he said something about meeting us here to-night, and as I had heard nothing from you I thought I would just ask. The slaves are so stupid about letters—not that I want very much to dine out. You see, I'm very busy just at this moment, and there's a Committee Meeting to-night for the O.S.P.F. (*She sighs.*) But one can't always think of oneself, and Brutus has been so depressed lately. He sleeps badly, and we've tried everything. The new Greek doctor has done him no good, and we've tried fomented eucalyptus and poppy soup, and the cold-water cure; but it all seems to make him worse, and the doctors say that what he wants is *society*, and we so seldom see any one.

LUCULLUS. I shall be quite delighted if you both could come to-night. (*He calls out*) Lucius. (*Enter* SLAVE.) Tell Æmilius at once we shall be two extra to dinner to-night; and tell him to get some more hoopoes' eggs.

PORTIA. Of course, I didn't mean to propose myself (*she laughs nervously*)—you mustn't think that; and have you really got room for us?

LUCULLUS. Oh, there's plenty of room. (*Pensively*) Do you like hoopoes' eggs?

PORTIA (*simpering*). Well, they're dreadfully indigestible, but I must say I never can resist a good hoopoe's egg. (*Getting up*) Then I can count on your patronage?

LUCULLUS. Certainly; is there a subscription?

PORTIO. Not for the patrons. You see——

LUCULLUS. Yes, I see.

PORTIA. Good-bye. Thank you so much.

Exit PORTIA. LUCULLUS *sees her to the door and returns.*

LUCULLUS (*pensively*). Brutus never drinks wine.

Enter SLAVE

THE SLAVE. The Queen of Egypt is here. Æmilius says it's too late to cook dinner for twelve now without spoiling it; he says we're one too many as it is, and that he can't get any more hoopoes' eggs, and that there won't be enough to go round.

LUCULLUS. Show the Queen in.

[*Exit* SLAVE.

Enter CLEOPATRA

CLEOPATRA. Don't get up, Lucullus; I'm not going to keep you a minute. I want to know if you could possibly dine with me to-night. I've got some dancing; a little Persian girl—so clever—she does a parakeet dance with live birds.

LUCULLUS. There's nothing I should like so much, dear Egypt; but I've got a dinner of my own. Do you want a man?

CLEOPATRA. I want *two* men, dreadfully.

LUCULLUS. I'll tell you who are coming—Mark Antony.

CLEOPATRA. I don't know him.

LUCULLUS. Cicero.

CLEOPATRA. I'm afraid he wouldn't do.

LUCULLUS. Brutus and his wife.

CLEOPATRA (*laughing*). They don't know me.

LUCULLUS. Catullus. Oh, I forgot Cæsar and his wife.

CLEOPATRA. Of course Cæsar would do beautifully, but I suppose you couldn't spare him.

LUCULLUS. To tell you the truth, I've got too many guests and not enough hoopoes' eggs to go round, but——

CLEOPATRA. Well, I happened to meet Cæsar quite by chance this morning, and he said that poor Calpurnia had got one of her headaches and was dying not to dine out, but you know how dear and unselfish she is. So if you should put them off, I think it would be rather a relief to *her*, and then Cæsar could just run in for a moment to my dinner.

LUCULLUS. Certainly; I'll say I've mistaken the date.

CLEOPATRA. That is charming of you; thank you so much. And you must come and dine quite quietly with me one night, and you might bring Mark Antony; I want to know him so much.

LUCULLUS. He's not interesting; he bolts his food.

CLEOPATRA. How funny! Just like Cæsar. Good-bye; I must fly.   [*Exit* CLEOPATRA.

Enter SLAVE

THE SLAVE. Clodia, the wife of Metellus Celer, wishes to see you.

LUCULLUS. Show her in, and tell Æmilius we shan't be two extra.

Enter CLODIA

CLODIA. It's too bad of me, Lucullus, to disturb you so early in the morning.

LUCULLUS. On the contrary——

CLODIA. What a charming room. (*Pointing to a statue of Hermes*) That's a Praxiteles, isn't it?

LUCULLUS. No; it's only a copy I had made by a little man at Puteoli.

CLODIA. I think it is wonderful.

LUCULLUS. It is clever.

CLODIA. You got my note?

LUCULLUS. Yes; I'm delighted you can come.

CLODIA. Well, that's just what I wanted to explain. Metellus says you've asked Catullus, and last night we were all dining with Pollio, and Catullus was there. Of course, I don't know him very well, but I've always been civil to him because of Metellus, who happens to like him. Well, last night he was so rude to my father-in-law that I don't feel as if I could meet him again to-night. I mean I don't think it would be right. Couldn't you put him off and say he made you thirteen?— otherwise I don't think I can come, and I wouldn't miss your dinner for worlds.

LUCULLUS (*enchanted*). Quite delighted, I assure you, to render you the smallest service. I will write at once. (*He scribbles two notes.*) Lucius! (*Enter a* SLAVE.) Take this note to Caius Valerius Catullus at once, and this one to the Queen of Egypt, and tell Æmilius we shall only be nine. (*To* CLODIA) I assure you it won't matter to him, as Cleopatra is giving a dinner to-night and is looking out for a man. I have written to tell her.

CLODIA. Cleopatra! Oh!

LUCULLUS. Yes; don't you like her?

CLODIA. Metellus hates Greeks; and I only just know her, but I do admire her. Metellus thinks she's so second-rate. I don't see it.

LUCULLUS. She's cultivated.

CLODIA. Yes; Greeks always are.

Enter a SLAVE *with a letter, which he gives to*
LUCULLUS

THE SLAVE. Waiting for an answer.

LUCULLUS. May I read this?

CLODIA. Please.

[LUCULLUS *opens the letter and looks at the signature.*

LUCULLUS. It's from one of my guests—Cynthia. I can't read it; I'm so short-sighted and I left my emerald upstairs.

CLODIA. Shall I read it for you?

LUCULLUS. That would be very kind.

CLODIA (*reads*). " DEAR LUCULLUS—I find I can come to dinner after all. I have just found a letter which has been going all over Rome for me for the last week, from the King of Nubia, who had asked me to-night (and of course it was a command), saying that his dinner is put off. So I shall be delighted to come to-night if I may.—CYNTHIA." That will just make you a woman over, won't it; but it will be all right if I don't come.

LUCULLUS. On the contrary——

CLODIA. Of course it will. You see, I may just as well come another night, and Metellus will come without me—husbands are always so much nicer without their wives. As a matter of fact, Metellus didn't much want me to come, because my throat's been rather bad lately, and he thinks I oughtn't to go out at night; so it all fits in. Good-bye, Lucullus.

Lucullus. Good-bye. (*Exit* Clodia.) She'll go to Cleopatra's—after all, food is wasted on women. Lucius!

Enter the Slave

The Slave. If you please, sir, Æmilius has killed himself!

Lucullus. Then who's going to cook the dinner?

The Slave. The head sauceman says he can manage the nightingales' tongues and the fish, but he's no experience of peacock.

Lucullus. Peacock! I should think not. He's not to touch the peacock. (*He walks up and down in great agitation, thinking.*) Tell the head sauceman —who is it—Balbus?

The Slave. Yes, sir.

Lucullus. Tell Balbus I will have dinner in my room an hour and a half before the other dinner. He can give soup, fish, pheasant, nightingales' tongues, the cold boar pie which was left from yesterday, and some hoopoes' eggs—and as for the dinner, you can send out for it. Send now to Varro's shop and order dinner for nine—eight courses—anything you like. Go at once. They may not be able to do it in time.

The Slave. If you please, sir, one of the slaves was over at Varro's this morning about the extra slaves to wait, and they said they had a dinner ordered and countermanded by Calpurnia on their hands.

Lucullus. That will do. But tell Balbus if my nightingales are not satisfactory he shall be impaled.

Curtain.

XV

THE STOIC'S DAUGHTER

SCENE.—*A room in the house of* BURRUS, *Prefect of the Prætorian Guards of Nero.* BURRUS *is discovered in an attitude of despondency.*

Enter a SLAVE

BURRUS. Well?

SLAVE. Caius Petronius would like to speak to you.

BURRUS. I will see him.

Enter C. PETRONIUS—PETRONIUS ARBITER, *middle-aged, but very elegant.*

PETRONIUS. Good morning. I've come about that dinner. The Emperor quite approves of the list of guests.

BURRUS. I don't suppose you wish me to come now.

PETRONIUS. Why not?

BURRUS. Well, after Lucius's—er—unfortunate escapade——

PETRONIUS. My dear fellow, I assure you that's not of the slightest consequence. If we had to be responsible for our sons' misdeeds life would become impossible. As it is, the Emperor, while sympathising with your feelings——

BURRUS. Please don't talk about it. You can understand how inexpressibly painful it is to me.

PETRONIUS. It might have been worse. He might have gone on the stage.

BURRUS. The gods spared us that. That would have killed Æmilia.

PETRONIUS. I suppose she feels it dreadfully.

BURRUS. It's not so much the thing she minds, but the family name being dragged into publicity —people making bets——

PETRONIUS. Yes, yes—but there's nothing to be done. After all, when all's said and done it is much less degrading to be a gladiator than an actor —or a charioteer. Piso's nephew is a charioteer, and Tigellinus's brother appeared on the stage for some charity.

BURRUS. I don't know what the world is coming to.

PETRONIUS. I suppose he'll drop it immediately. Then I should send him abroad for a little, and the world will forget all about it. These things are forgotten so quickly. After all, boys will be boys. Believe me, young men must sow their wild oats, and the sooner they get it over the better. Well, please give my respects to Æmilia, and I can count on you for certain for the fifteenth?

BURRUS. I shall come without fail.

[*Exit* PETRONIUS.

Enter ÆMILIA—BURRUS'S *wife*

ÆMILIA. Well? What did he say?

BURRUS. Nothing, practically. The Emperor doesn't seem to have said anything.

ÆMILIA. But do you mean to say you haven't arranged anything?

BURRUS. What about? The dinner-party?

ÆMILIA. Dinner-party, indeed! I mean about Lucius not appearing at the Games again.

BURRUS. No, I haven't. What is there to arrange?

ÆMILIA. You really are too helpless. You must get him banished, of course—just for a short time.

BURRUS. I didn't like to—but I'll write to Seneca.

ÆMILIA. Seneca's no use. Write to Petronius. He'll arrange it without any fuss.

BURRUS. I hardly like——

ÆMILIA. If Lucius appears once more in the circus as a gladiator I shall open my veins in my bath.

BURRUS. Oh, well, of course, if you insist——

ÆMILIA. Yes, I do insist.

Enter a SLAVE

SLAVE. Lucius Annæus Seneca, and Annæus Serenus wish to see you.

BURRUS. Show them in.

Enter LUCIUS A. SENECA, *and* A. SERENUS

[*Exit* SLAVE.

SENECA. I've only just heard the news, or else I would have come sooner.

SERENUS. And I had no idea until Seneca told me.

BURRUS. I suppose it's all over Rome by now.

SENECA. You mustn't take these things to heart.

ÆMILIA. It's all very well for you to talk, Seneca; you haven't got a son.

SENECA. I would esteem it a privilege to be

visited by troubles of this nature. It is only the noblest souls that the gods plague with such disasters in order that, tempered by affliction, the true steel, emerging triumphant from the trial, may serve as an example to mankind.

SERENUS. Not being a stoic, Burrus, I take a different view of the incident. I consider that man is born to enjoy himself, and that the opportunities of enjoyment are rare and far between. Life is monotonous. If your son finds a relaxation from the tediousness of existence in fighting as a gladiator, by all means let him continue to do so. It is a profession which calls forth many of the noblest qualities of man.

ÆMILIA. But think of the family, Serenus. Think of us, of my sisters, my sisters-in-law, my cousins; think of my husband and the harm that it may do him professionally.

SENECA. Vain thoughts, I assure you, Æmilia. A man's merit depends on the aspirations of his soul and not on the idle gossip of his relations.

SERENUS. All one's relations are liars. It is much better that they should say your son is a gladiator who fights in public—which is true—than that they should say he is a drunkard who drinks in secret, which would be untrue. They would no doubt say that, had they no other food for gossip.

ÆMILIA. But Lucius never drinks. He had never given us a day's anxiety until this.

BURRUS. He got all the prizes at school.

ÆMILIA. He was working so hard to become an officer.

SERENUS. Ah! Over-education, I see. I assure you the whole matter does not signify.

ÆMILIA. It is breaking his father's heart.

BURRUS. I shall never hold up my head in public.

SENECA. Come, Burrus, think of Brutus, and what he had to endure from his son.

SERENUS. Yes, and think of the many Roman sons who have killed their fathers.

SENECA. In every evil, in every misfortune there is always a seed of consolation. You must, of course, deal kindly with him, but firmly, and I am convinced he will listen to reason.

ÆMILIA. He wouldn't listen to us at all. We all tried our best to dissuade him—except his cousin Lesbia. Heartless woman! It was entirely her fault.

BURRUS. He shall never cross this threshold again as long as I live.

SENECA. Set a noble example of forgiveness, Burrus, and the world will be grateful to you.

BURRUS. I will never set eyes upon him again. He has disgraced himself and his family for ever. There are certain stains of dishonour which can never be effaced.

Enter a SLAVE

SLAVE. Paulina, the wife of Seneca, is here. She wishes to speak to you.

SENECA. My wife! What can she want?

BURRUS. Show her in

[*Exit* SLAVE.

Enter PAULINA

PAULINA. Forgive me, Burrus, for forcing my way in—they said you were not at home to any visitors—but it is a matter of life and death—and

I must speak to Seneca. (*To* SENECA) I have been hunting for you the whole morning, and it's by the merest chance I found out you had come here.

SENECA. What is it?

PAULINA. A terrible catastrophe has befallen us.

SENECA. My Greek vases!

PAULINA. No, it's nothing to do with your horrible collections.

SENECA. Then don't you think we had better go home and discuss the matter in private?

PAULINA. No, I want Burrus's help.

SENECA. What can have happened?

PAULINA. It's Julia.

SENECA. I suppose she's run away with some one.

PAULINA. Oh no; it's far worse than that.

SENECA. You mean——

PAULINA. I don't mean anything. I mean she has disgraced us all.

SERENUS. These little affairs blow over so quickly.

PAULINA. But you don't understand—you will never believe it. The girl has become a Christian.

SENECA. A Christian!

BURRUS. No!

ÆMILIA. My poor Paulina!

SERENUS. Curious!

BURRUS. She must have been got hold of by the Jews.

ÆMILIA. They are terribly cunning; and people say they're everywhere, and yet one doesn't see them.

SERENUS. But surely there is nothing irretrievable about this. As long as nobody knows about it, what does it signify?

SENECA. You don't understand. It's a matter of principle; I could not possibly harbour a daughter under my roof whom I knew to be a traitor to the State.

SERENUS. It is annoying.

PAULINA. But you don't know the worst: she has gone to prison.

SENECA (*very angry*). Well, I hope you will let her know that she shall never come back to our home as long as she lives. Her conduct is not only immoral, but it is immodest. It is inspired solely and simply by a passion for self-advertisement. It is this modern craze for publicity which is the ruin of our children; she is bitten by this same passion for notoriety which—you will excuse me saying so, Burrus—led your son to be a gladiator. I call it vulgar, tawdry, Byzantine, hysterical, and essentially un-Roman.

SERENUS. But surely, my dear Seneca, nobody can think it amusing to go to prison? Think of the risk.

SENECA. I beg your pardon. People of her class risk nothing. They have got a morbid craze for new sensations.

SERENUS. Rather disagreeable sensations, aren't they? To be eaten by a tiger, for instance?

SENECA. There's no question of that. It's only the worst criminals who are treated like that. Am I not right, Burrus?

BURRUS. Perfectly. A purely religious offender is immediately released on making the mere outward sign of allegiance to the State. An oath is not even required.

PAULINA. Well, that's just what I've come

about. The child is in prison, and it appears—it is very foolish and obstinate of her, but Julia always was an obstinate child—that she refuses to fulfil the necessary formality, sacrifice, or whatever it is. So I thought I would come to you, Burrus, and ask you just to say a word to the prison authorities, and then she could be let out—quite quietly, of course. Nobody need know about it.

BURRUS. My dear lady, you know how gladly I would do anything in the world to be of use to you. But in this case—and I am sure you will understand—I cannot see my way; indeed it is quite impossible for me to take any action. You see, Petronius's cousin was released three weeks ago, and smuggled out of the country, and the demagogues got hold of it and complained to the Emperor, who—courting popularity as usual—said it was not to occur again. So you see in what an awkward position we are placed. We can't make these distinctions simply between people of position and others——

PAULINA. But it's always done.

BURRUS. That's just why it can't be done this time. The Emperor is extremely annoyed at people of good family having anything to do with those horrible Christians, and he's determined to stamp this mania out. But all she has got to do is to sacrifice——

PAULINA. But you don't realise how obstinate the girl is.

Enter LESBIA, *a lovely gay woman, about twenty-five.*

LESBIA. Good morning, good morning. I've

got some places for the Games, and Lucius comes on at three. You *must* see him fight. He's too wonderful. And it's horrible of you not to go and see him, and then they're going to throw *all* the Christians to the lions directly afterwards, so you must come.

CURTAIN.

XVI

AFTER EURIPIDES' "ELECTRA"

SCENE.—*A room in the house of* CINYRAS, *at Athens.*
Reclining on couches round the tables are
SOCRATES, ALCANDER (*a man about Athens*),
DEMETRIUS (*a critic*), XENOCLES (*a play-*
wright), ANTAGORAS (*an important official*),
NAUCYDES (*a soldier*), HELIODORE (*wife of*
CINYRAS), *and her friends,* LYCORIS, TIMARETA,
NICYLLA, *and* HEGESO.

HELIODORE. Euripides has promised to come;
but we won't wait for him. I don't know what you
feel, but I'm very hungry.

NAUCYDES. So am I. Makes one hungry, don't
you know—that kind of thing. Splendid show.

LYCORIS. What I say is, it's too long. It
lasted nearly all day. If he had made it about half
as long, it would be just as beautiful, and much
more enjoyable for us. Of course, I don't pretend
to be a judge, but I do say it's too long.

CINYRAS. Much the best thing is to do as I do
and not go to the play at all.

LYCORIS. No, I like a *good* play. But I don't
care for Diophantus' acting. It's just the same
with Tityus. What I say is, Diophantus is always
Diophantus and Tityus is always Tityus.

DEMETRIUS. But surely the business of the actor is never to let his personality change?

NICYLLA. What did you think of the play, Demetrius?

DEMETRIUS. I am afraid I must not tell you that until my opinions are published. It wouldn't be fair on the author.

NICYLLA. And what did you think, Socrates?

SOCRATES. I admired it immensely.

HEGESO. I thought it wonderful. I loved the story. I loved Clytæmnestra's clothes, that wonderful, dirty, wine-stained dress, and Electra's pale, shivering, stone-cold mask; and Orestes was such a darling. So mad, and distraught, and rebellious.

HELIODORE. I thought it was marvellous.

NICYLLA. I think it's so much better than Sophocles' *Electra*.

ALCANDER. It's very clever, of course; brilliantly clever; but it's not a play. It's really only a discussion.

HEGESO. But I was thrilled by the story and so frightened.

TIMARETA. You know, it's not the story. It's the acting. Apollodorus told me it's the acting. It's wonderful. It's felt. I felt it.

LYCORIS. I must say, I don't like that sort of play. I think it leaves a nasty taste in one's mouth and one doesn't quite know why. I know it's very clever.

NICYLLA. Oh, Lycoris, how old-fashioned of you! Now don't you think Electra was right, Socrates, to kill her mother?

SOCRATES. We'll ask Euripides that when he comes. My business is to ask questions——

NAUCYDES (*aside to* HELIODORE). And a great nuisance he is, too, with his questions.

SOCRATES. And not to answer them.

NAUCYDES (*aside to* HELIODORE). I don't believe he knows what the answers are.

NICYLLA. But don't you think, Demetrius, that a girl is justified in taking the law into her hands in such very exceptional circumstances; or do you think a girl's first duty is to her mother?

ANTAGORAS. I think she deserved a good whipping, if you ask me. However, it's not the story I object to. I mean, we all know the story, and we're quite ready to see a new play on the subject, as long as it's treated reverently and decently; but one never knows with Euripides when he's serious, or whether he's laughing in his sleeve the whole time or not. Now I like Æschylus.

XENOCLES. Poor Euripides! He's shot his bolt.

NICYLLA. Do you think he's played out?

LYCORIS. What I say is this, that Clytæmnestra thoroughly deserved to die, but Electra wasn't the person to kill her, and that as she did kill her mother she ought to have been punished.

TIMARETA. It was Fate, that's what it was. Apollodorus told me it was all Fate.

HEGESO. Yes, and she was so sad, so miserable; she couldn't bear doing it. She *loved* her mother, although her mother had been so unkind, and turned her out of that beautiful house into a cold cruel hut, and only a herdsman to talk to. Don't you agree, Naucydes, with me that Electra was cruelly treated? She couldn't help it, could she?

NAUCYDES. Rather an awkward case, don't you

know. Sort of fix when everything you do's wrong. (*He laughs loudly.*)

HEGESO. And wasn't the music too heavenly?

ALCANDER. It's like the play—clever; but it isn't music, any more than the play's a play.

ANTAGORAS. I couldn't make head or tail of it— but then I'm not musical.

HEGESO. Didn't you love those divine little screams, like a saw cutting ice, and the noise the cymbals made, like slippery sandals rushing down a marble mountain?

NICYLLA. What did you think of the music, Demetrius?

DEMETRIUS. There are no ideas in it, and it's very thin; there's no colour in it either, but a certain amount of clever arabesque work.

NICYLLA. Don't you think music acts on one's sub-conscious superself without one's noticing it? When I hear certain kinds of music I go quite mad, and sometimes when I hear music I feel as if I could understand everything. I am sure you agree with me, Socrates. And now, *do* tell me : Does music have an Apolline or a Dionysic effect on you? Sometimes it has a Dionysic effect on me and sometimes an Apolline.

SOCRATES. What is music, Nicylla? If you can answer me that, I will tell you the nature of its effect on me.

NICYLLA. Music is the language of the soul. It is to man what the perfume is to the flower.

ANTAGORAS. Music's a nuisance.

DEMETRIUS. Not necessarily; but it is often an interruption.

ALCANDER. And sometimes an accompaniment.

LYCORIS. Yes, as in the play to-day. What I say is, all this new music isn't music, but noise.

ANTAGORAS. I agree with you; it oughtn't to be allowed.

DEMETRIUS. But isn't all music noise?

HEGESO. Yes; delicious, heavenly noises, all caught like tame mice and put in chains and made to be obedient.

HELIODORE. Don't let's discuss the music till we've finished talking about the play. Now, Xenocles thinks that Euripides is played out.

XENOCLES. Euripides has talent, but he is essentially mediocre; his verses are vulgar and facile. However, I've no doubt the sausage-sellers enjoy his plays. It is the kind of thing which would appeal to them. And they say the Barbarians find them extraordinarily profound.

NICYLLA. Now, that's one of your paradoxes, Xenocles. How brilliant he is, isn't he?

TIMARETA. Apollodorus says his characters are too natural. They are just what one sees every day.

ANTAGORAS. Good gracious! I hope not.

NICYLLA. Now, Socrates, I know you admire Euripides, and I always have admired him. I always said from the first that he was far the greatest playwright we'd ever had. I want to know what Xenocles admires.

XENOCLES. Well, there's Agathon, but no one else.

NICYLLA. And I'm sure you don't admire Sophocles?

XENOCLES. The gods forbid.

DEMETRIUS. His work is quite dead. I believe his plays are still admired in Thrace.

NAUCYDES. I saw one the other day, and I'm afraid I liked it.

NICYLLA. Oh, Naucydes, how can you say such a thing? They're so empty. There's no soul in them. No world-sympathy. No atmospheric intuition. Nothing cosmic. And then they say his verses are all wrong. Aren't they, Xenocles?

XENOCLES. Sophocles undoubtedly wrote some good lines, but his philosophy is childish. It is essentially Mid-Athenian.

HEGESO. Oh, I adore Mid-Athenian things. I've had a room furnished in the Mid-Athenian style with archaic busts; you can't think how quaint and charming it looks.

HELIODORE. Won't you have a little more partridge, Hegeso?

HEGESO. No, thank you, dear. I never touch food at this time in the evening. I can only eat a little parsley and mint in the morning.

HELIODORE. I'm sure you must be hungry after all we've gone through. I confess I cried like a child.

TIMARETA. That's what it is—Euripides is so pathetic. He's not great and he's not mystic, but he's pathetic. He touches one just here. (*She points to her throat.*) Apollodorus told me he's pathetic. He's got bathos.

HEGESO. I felt so sorry for Clytæmnestra. I was miserable when she screamed. I jumped up in my seat and cried: " I can't bear it, I can't bear it; they're killing Clytæmnestra." And Callias, who was sitting next to me, was so cross. (*She helps herself to a quail.*) It has been a wonderful day.

HELIODORE.   Wonderful!   I've never been through anything like it before.

NICYLLA.   I felt as if my soul had escaped and was just floating in mid-ether between one world and another;   between the two gates, don't you know.

TIMARETA.   I was moved, that's what it was—moved.   I felt like—as if I were at a funeral—a State funeral, with music and torches.

ALCANDER.   Yes, it was certainly a fine performance.

NAUCYDES.   By Zeus, yes!

DEMETRIUS.   I don't mind saying that I was interested.

HEGESO.   I shall never get over it, never.   I feel as if it had all happened to me.   (*She helps herself to another quail.*)

Enter a SLAVE

THE SLAVE.   Euripides has sent to say he is very sorry he can't come to supper.   He is too tired.

SOCRATES.   I am afraid I must leave you.   I have some pupils waiting for me at home.

HELIODORE.   Oh, don't go, Socrates.   I haven't spoken to you at all, and I have got so many things to say to you.

SOCRATES.   I'm afraid I must go.   Farewell, and a thousand thanks for your kind hospitality.

DEMETRIUS.   And I'm afraid I must go.   I've got to write about the play.

[*Exeunt* SOCRATES *and* DEMETRIUS.

HELIODORE.   I must say I do think it's rather thoughtless of Euripides to throw me over at the last minute.   I do think he might have let me know.

You see, Socrates only came because of Euripides. And you see what happens the moment he hears he's not coming—he goes.

XENOCLES. He always does that. He's spoilt. I told you he was overrated.

HELIODORE. I don't mind personally a bit. I don't happen to care for him; but I have asked thirty people to come in afterwards to meet him, and I do think it's selfish.

LYCORIS. I could tell from his play he was selfish.

TIMARETA. He's no heart, that's what it is. He's heartless. Just like Electra—heartless.

HELIODORE. But I do think Socrates might have stayed.

XENOCLES. Don't you understand why he's gone? He didn't want to tell Euripides how bad he thought the play was!

NICYLLA. Do you mean he really thinks it bad?

XENOCLES. I'm convinced of it.

ANTAGORAS. It's much worse than bad; it's undermining.

ALCANDER. Yes, I'm afraid it's a failure.

HEGESO. Oh no, don't say that, because I did so love it.

HELIODORE. I never liked Euripides.

NICYLLA. I told you he was finished. I'm never wrong. I knew it was all a mistake.

XENOCLES. He means well.

ANTAGORAS. No, he doesn't; that's just it.

LYCORIS. What I say is, that those kinds of plays do harm.

ANTAGORAS. The man's an atheist.

LYCORIS. He's a scoffer.

ANTAGORAS. But Socrates is far worse than he is.

NICYLLA. Oh, he's such a bore.

HEGESO. I love his little snub nose.

HELIODORE. I shall never ask them again.

ALCANDER. Tiresome people.

LYCORIS. What I say is, people like Socrates and Euripides ought to be put in prison.

NICYLLA. Especially Socrates.

ANTAGORAS. So he will be, or else my name's not Antagoras. He only deserves one thing, and that's capital punishment.

HEGESO. Poor little Socrates! But I hope you'll let Euripides off.

ANTAGORAS. He doesn't count; he's only a playwright.

CURTAIN.

XVII

JASON AND MEDEA

Scene.—*A room in the house of* Jason, *looking on to garden, at Corinth. Discovered :* Jason *ana* Glauce.

Jason. I think you really had better go. She may be in any minute now.

Glauce. Very well; but you promise to tell her to-day ?

Jason. I swear.

Glauce. It's all very well, but you said that yesterday.

Jason. Yes, and I would have told her yesterday, only I was interrupted——

Glauce. I know; the only thing I say is, you must tell her to-day and do it nicely, because I shouldn't like poor little Medea to be hurt.

Jason. No, of course not. Good-bye.

Glauce. Good-bye. Then to-morrow at eleven, at the Creon Institute.

Jason. Very well, at eleven.

Glauce. And then we might—no.

Jason. What ?

Glauce. Nothing. I was only thinking we might have some food at the " Golden Fleece," *downstairs*.

Jason. The whole of Corinth would see us.

GLAUCE. There is never a soul downstairs, and I don't see now that it much matters.

JASON. It's a pity to make oneself conspicuous; your father——

GLAUCE. You know best, but I should have thought——

JASON. That's Medea coming through the garden.

GLAUCE. To-morrow, at eleven.

JASON. Yes — yes — to-morrow. (GLAUCE *goes out L.*)

Enter MEDEA *from the garden*

MEDEA. I can't get any one for dinner to-morrow night. We want somebody amusing.

JASON (*wearily*). Would Orpheus do?

MEDEA. We've got too many heroes as it is. And then, if Orpheus comes, we shall be obliged to ask him to play.

JASON. What about Castor and Pollux?

MEDEA. Heroes again—and I think it's a mistake to ask brothers together.

JASON. Heracles is staying at Corinth.

MEDEA. He would do beautifully.

JASON. I'm not sure he would do. He doesn't get on with Admetus.

MEDEA. Why not? Admetus ought to be very grateful.

JASON. For bringing back his wife from the grave?

MEDEA. Yes, of course.

JASON. Of course. (JASON *looks pensive.*)

MEDEA. Then we shall want another woman.

JASON. How would Ariadne do?

MEDEA. What are you thinking of? Theseus is coming.

JASON. I thought all that had entirely blown over.

MEDEA. We want an unmarried woman, if possible.

JASON. I don't know any one.

MEDEA. Do you think we could get King Creon's daughter by herself? She's so pretty. I mean Glauce.

JASON (*blushing scarlet*). I don't think—er—no —you see—we can't very well.

MEDEA. Why not?

JASON. She's a girl.

MEDEA. She goes everywhere. She doesn't count as a girl.

JASON. Then we should have to ask King Creon.

MEDEA. No, Alcestis will bring her. That will do beautifully. I'll send a message at once.

JASON. For the sake of the gods, do nothing of the kind.

MEDEA. But she'll do beautifully.

JASON. You don't understand. You see, King Creon has—he's—well, I don't quite know how to say it.

MEDEA. What *do* you mean?

JASON. Well, it's very awkward. The fact is, King Creon has approached me politically—about something——

MEDEA. What has that got to do with asking Glauce?

JASON. No, nothing, of course, except that we should have to ask him.

MEDEA. I've already told you that it's unnecessary.

JASON (*firmly*). I shouldn't dream of asking her without her father, and we can't ask him.

MEDEA. Why not?

JASON. Oh, because he never does dine out.

MEDEA. I'm sure he would come here.

JASON. It's impossible. You see, to tell you the truth—I've been meaning to tell you this for some time, only I've never had the opportunity— the King is rather severe about you.

MEDEA. Severe! How?

JASON. Well, you see, he's old-fashioned, and he doesn't consider our marriage is a marriage.

MEDEA. We were married in the temple of Aphrodite What more does he want?

JASON. He doesn't consider that a girl's marriage is valid when it is made without the consent of her parents; and your poor dear father, you know, was most unreasonable.

MEDEA. Papa being silly has got nothing to do with it. When a man and a woman are married in a temple, with the proper rites, they are man and wife. Nothing can ever alter the fact.

JASON. Yes, but it's not only that. Creon goes much farther than that. He made me certain revelations concerning some family business which, I must say, surprised me immensely.

MEDEA. What family business?

JASON. Well, it appears that soon after I started for Colchis my father entered into secret negotiations with King Creon, and signed an offensive and defensive alliance with him, with the object of safeguarding himself against Pelias. The word-alliance remained secret. But at a State banquet Creon laid great stress on the friendship between himself and the Æolidæ, and brought in the words " friendly understanding " several times. Now in the treaty, which was drawn up and published, to mask the alliance, there were several secret clauses. One of them concerned the Sardine Fisheries in the Isthmus of Corinth, and the other—well—er, my marriage.

MEDEA. Your marriage.

JASON. Yes, it is extraordinary, isn't it? It appears that during my absence, and without my being consulted in any way whatsoever, I was formally married, by proxy, of course, to Creon's daughter Glauce—who was at that time a mere child. It was further settled that as soon as she was grown up, the marriage should be announced and the King should publicly adopt me as his heir.

MEDEA. No wonder he was annoyed at your having married me.

JASON. Well, you see, he isn't annoyed at that, because he says our marriage wasn't valid.

MEDEA. Not in the eyes of the law, perhaps; but I am sure Aphrodite would not only be pained, but extremely angry if we cancelled vows which were made in her temple.

JASON. No, that's just it. It appears he consulted all the oracles and the priestesses, and the Pythonesses, and they all say that our marriage is not only illegal, but positively criminal, and that my lawful wife, both in the eyes of man and of the gods, is Glauce.

MEDEA. And my children?

JASON. Well, about the children, opinion was

slightly divided; but they inclined to think that, if I adopted them, they would be considered legitimate.

MEDEA. Legitimate! I should hope so. But what did you say to Creon? I suppose you told him you were very sorry, but that it couldn't be helped. (*She laughs.*) Poor Glauce! It's a shame to make a girl so ridiculous.

JASON. I don't think you quite realise how seriously Creon regards the matter.

MEDEA. I don't care an obol what he thinks. What I want to be told is how you told him what you think.

JASON. Of course, I said that I felt highly flattered.

MEDEA. But that you were married already.

JASON. No, it was no use saying that, because —as I've already said twice—he does not think our marriage counts.

MEDEA. Then what did you say?

JASON. Oh, I said I would lay the matter before you, and trust to your great good sense.

MEDEA. Do you mean to say that you did not give him to understand that the whole thing was altogether mad, absurd, and utterly preposterous?

JASON. How could I? After all, he is the King; and, moreover, he is backed up by all the legal and hieratic authorities. I could do nothing. I was quite helpless, quite defenceless. I simply had to incline myself before his higher authority.

MEDEA. Oh, I see; you accepted, in fact.

[*She reflects a moment.*

JASON. I didn't exactly accept. But what else could I do?

MEDEA. No, of course, it's quite simple. You said that our marriage didn't count; you would be delighted to marry Glauce.

JASON. I didn't use the word " delighted."

MEDEA. " Highly honoured," perhaps?

JASON. Something like that.

MEDEA. So you are engaged to be married? (*Without any irony in her voice*) Well, I congratulate you.

JASON. Not engaged. You see, the King——

MEDEA (*cheerfully*). I know. You mean you are married to Glauce theoretically, and now you are going to make the marriage a reality.

JASON (*intensely relieved at there not being a scene*). How clearly you put things !

MEDEA. I'm delighted for your sake. She's a charming girl, and I am sure she will make you very happy.

JASON. But, Medea, what about you? You quite understand that I am ready to give up the whole thing unless you are quite sure you don't mind?

MEDEA. My dear Jason, why should I mind? My only wish is that you should be happy.

JASON. I'm afraid that's impossible. I need hardly say I am not in the least in love with Glauce.

MEDEA. Of course not. But what about my children?

JASON. Ah, there's the difficulty. The King says they will have to remain with me. But you will be able to come and see them whenever you like.

MEDEA. Oh, I see.

JASON. The King is very particular about children being brought up by their father. He thinks women make them into mollycoddles.

MEDEA. Yes, of course. I suppose, since the marriage ceremony has already been performed, you won't have to go through it again.

JASON. It's unnecessary; but I'm sorry to say the King wishes it.

MEDEA. Then I suppose it will be soon. I shall leave Corinth as soon as my things can be packed.

JASON. The King wants the ceremony to be this week; but you mustn't inconvenience yourself in any way.

MEDEA (*smiling*). No, I won't. Good-bye for the moment. I am going out to buy Glauce a present.   [*She goes out.*

JASON *walks up to a flower-pot and takes a lily from it. He speaks into the lily :* Is that oooo Corinth Wall? Darling, is that you? Yes, it's all over. She's taken it wonderfully. No. Yes, certainly ask her to stay later. Creon Institute to-morrow at eleven. Good-bye, darling.

CURTAIN.

XVIII

MEDEA GOES SHOPPING

SCENE.—*A Shop in Corinth. Discovered* GLAUCE *looking at some models and* MEDEA *looking at something else.*

MEDEA (*to* GLAUCE). Is there nobody in this shop who can attend to me? I've been waiting a quarter of an hour. (GLAUCE *stares at her icily.*) Oh, I beg your pardon! Oh, it's darling Glauce. How funny! You know how shortsighted I am. You are just the person I wanted to see. Jason has been telling me. I do congratulate you. I think it's such an excellent plan. You see I never could have left the poor old thing. It would have been too great a shame. You must be kind to him and see that he has his cup of goat's milk, *boiled*, you know, *every* night, and only a pint of Chian wine in the evening. All the doctors say that for his age he's wonderfully well preserved. But he *must* be careful.

GLAUCE. I'm afraid I must go.

MEDEA. You mustn't let me be in the way. I can come any time.

GLAUCE. Thank you very much. I have seen everything I wanted to see.

MEDEA. Of course, darling, you get everything from Carthage. What a lovely frock that is! So Punic.

GLAUCE. It's very old. My maid just threw it together. Good-bye.

MEDEA. Good-bye, darling.

[*Exit* GLAUCE.

Enter a SALESMAN

MEDEA. I want something for a wedding present for a friend. Something she can wear in the evening. Not too expensive. But something that will look nice and make an effect.

SALESMAN. Certainly, Madam. We have some very nice Carthage models.

MEDEA. I'm afraid I can't run to that.

SALESMAN. Is it a dress you want, Madam?

MEDEA. No, not a dress, a cloak. Something to wear for going out to a feast, a " Terpsichore " Exodos.

SALESMAN. Yes, Madam. An amphitheatre cloak. (*Showing a cloak.*) This is very much worn now. Halcyon feathers and petals of asphodel. Quite a novelty. The Queen of Crete ordered six of them yesterday. Just the thing for Olympia. Stylish without being loud. And a real bargain, thirteen talents. Can be worn in the daytime or in the evening, and suitable for half mourning.

MEDEA. I don't want mourning. It's for a wedding present.

SALESMAN. I quite understand, Madam. We've a very nice peplos in orange pungee. Indian silk is very fashionable just now.

MEDEA. It's too young-looking.

SALESMAN. Yes, Madam. A second marriage, perhaps. We've the very thing. Here's a chiton. Our own model. Persian muslin. We call it the Amazon.

MEDEA. I don't want a riding habit.

L

SALESMAN. We've a very nice chlamys, Madam; cerulean silk, trimmed with imitation pearls.

MEDEA. How much is that?

SALESMAN. Eleven talents, Madam. It's reduced. We were asking twelve for it.

MEDEA. It doesn't seem very fresh.

SALESMAN. It's slightly shop-soiled, and on account of that I could take something off. I could let you have it, Madam, for ten talents, thirty drachmas, and seventy-five obols.

MEDEA. I'm afraid all these models are too expensive. I think I'll buy the stuff and run it up at home. Can I see some stuff?

SALESMAN. For a peplos or a chiton, Madam?

MEDEA. I think it had better be a chiton.

SALESMAN. Quite so, Madam. Stockinette or crêpe?

MEDEA. Not stockinette.

SALESMAN. This, Madam, is a beautiful material, just come in, called Golden Fleece taffetas.

MEDEA. That wouldn't do at all.

SALESMAN. We've some very nice Etrurian muslin.

MEDEA. Can I see it?

SALESMAN. Certainly, Madam (*throws out the stuff on the counter*).

MEDEA. How much is that?

SALESMAN. It's really given away, Madam, ten drachmas a yard.

MEDEA. It's too flimsy.

SALESMAN. Perhaps, Madam. Not quite important enough for an occasion. Now, here's a new material, just in from Athens. Georgette, called after the Gorgon sisters. We have it in mauve, pink, and grey. The Medusa shade is very much sought after.

MEDEA. That would do all right for the day, but I don't think it would show by lamplight.

SALESMAN. We can see in a moment, Madam. I will darken the room.

[*The room is darkened but for one small lamp. The* SALESMAN *waves the material in front of the lamp.*

MEDEA. It's flat by lamplight. The wedding torches would kill it.

SALESMAN. Here's something from Africa, Madam Moorish kraipnos, it's called. Just the thing for a wedding, not too young, and yet quite bridal.

MEDEA. How much is it?

SALESMAN. That would be *for you*, Madam, as you're an old customer, fifty drachmas a yard.

MEDEA. Double width?

SALESMAN. Thirty-one inches, Madam.

MEDEA. It's very dear.

SALESMAN. We have some cheap organdies, Madam. White and crushed arbutus.

MEDEA. That would be too light.

SALESMAN. We've some beautiful " charmatodes " satin, or some cream tussore, or a saffron bombychine, very hymeneal.

MEDEA. I suppose the " Sphinx " kraipnos is very expensive?

SALESMAN (*showing some*). Not at all, Madam. This only runs to thirty drachmas a yard, double width.

MEDEA. That would do, but I don't like the colour.

SALESMAN. We could do it you in magenta and golden—I mean in *silver* fleece shades.

MEDEA. I think I'll have it dyed. I'll send you the dye. I've an excellent precious dye at home, made of Centaur's blood, by a little man. Could you use that?

SALESMAN. Certainly, Madam. The " Nessus " preparation, I suppose? It is, of course, Madam, as you know, highly inflammable.

MEDEA. But I suppose it wouldn't be very dangerous unless worn next to the skin?

SALESMAN. No, Madam, not unless worn next to the skin. But if it was worn next to the skin it would certainly blister—as it's for a jumper—I mean a chiton——

MEDEA. I'm not sure I shall make it into a jumper, and it's for a chilly person.

SALESMAN. Quite so, Madam. How many yards may I put up for you, Madam?

MEDEA. Three and a half, please.

SALESMAN. I'll just measure it for you, Madam. (*He measures it.*) Very nice weather we've been having lately.

MEDEA. The climate's so changeable, one never knows what to wear.

SALESMAN. That was a dreadful thing about poor Mr. Phæthon.

MEDEA. Dreadful, but if inexperienced whips will drive the sun——

SALESMAN. Exactly so, Madam. Nothing seems to get any safer. Is it to be entered to account, or shall I send it?

MEDEA. Yes, please enter it, and send it, as soon as you have dyed it, to Queen Medea, the Palace.

SALESMAN. Yes, Your Majesty. (*Writes down and reads as he writes*), Her Majesty, the Queen of Corinth.

MEDEA. No, no, no. Queen Medea, the Palace, Corinth.

CURTAIN.

XIX

KING ALFRED AND THE NEAT-HERD

SCENE.—*Interior of a* NEAT-HERD'S *hut, near the river Parret, in Somersetshire.*

Enter a NEAT-HERD, *followed by* KING ALFRED, *who is miserably clad and shivering from cold ; he carries a bow and a few broken arrows. A log fire is burning smokily in a corner of the hut.*

THE NEAT-HERD (*scratching the back of his head*). Reckon t' old 'ooman 'ull be baack zoon.

THE KING.   We are very hungry.

THE NEAT-HERD.   Reckon t' old 'ooman 'ull be baack zoon.   She be a baaking.

[*The* KING *sits down by the fire and warms himself.   Enter the* NEAT-HERD'S WIFE *with much noise and bustle ; she carries a batch of newly-kneaded loaves on a tray, which she puts down in front of the fire.   The* NEAT-HERD *says something to her in an undertone ; she mutters something in answer about "strange folk."   Then she goes up to the* KING.

THE NEAT-HERD'S WIFE.   If ye be a-staying here ye must make yournself useful.

THE KING (*rising and bowing politely*).   We should be delighted to do anything in our power.

THE NEAT-HERD'S WIFE (*looking at the* KING *with distrust, and talking very quickly*). I'ze warrant ye be strange in these parts. (*To her husband*) I reckon we've no time to see after strange folk. We all be hungry, and it's a mercy we've still got a morsel of bread in the house to keep the children from ztark ztarving, and that's zo. But if he'll look to t' baatch whiles I zee to t' cows, maybe ee'll get a morsel for his pains. (*To the* KING) Now do ee be zure, stranger, ye turn the baatch when they're done a one side.

THE KING (*who has only partially understood what she has said*). We shall be delighted. (*He bows.*)

THE NEAT-HERD'S WIFE (*to her husband*). I reckon he do be daaft.

THE NEAT-HERD. He's no daaft; he be strange.

THE NEAT-HERD'S WIFE. See ee turn the baatch.

THE NEAT-HERD. Oo! AR!

[*The* NEAT-HERD'S WIFE *goes out and slams the door.*

[*The* KING *sits again by the fire and begins to mend his broken arrows; after a pause:*

THE KING. Do you care for verse?—poetry?

[*The* NEAT-HERD *scratches the back of his head, and after reflecting for some time:*

THE NEAT-HERD. Oo! AR!

THE KING. Then we will repeat to you a few little things—mere trifles—we composed in the marshes during our leisure hours. (*He looks pensively upwards.*)

There are clouds in the sky,
    I'm afraid it will rain.
I cannot think why
There are clouds in the sky.
Had I wings, I would fly
    To the deserts of Spain.
There are clouds in the sky,
    I'm afraid it will rain.

THE KING. That is a triolet.

THE NEAT-HERD. Oo! AR!

THE KING. Here is another. It was written in dejection.

I've had nothing to eat
    For nearly two days.
It's beginning to sleet,
I've had nothing to eat;
Neither oatmeal nor wheat,
    Nor millet nor maize.
I've had nothing to eat
    For nearly two days.

That is also a triolet—perhaps not quite so successful. (*He looks at the* NEAT-HERD *inquiringly.*)

THE NEAT-HERD. Oo! AR!

THE KING. We will now repeat to you a sonnet. It is adapted from Boethius. It is called " Suspiria."

[*He passes his hand through his hair and looks upward towards the right.*

I used to sit upon an ivory chair,
And wear a jewelled crown upon my head;
Fine linen draped in folds my carven bed,
With myrrh I used to smooth and scent my hair.

I used to play upon a golden harp,
And every one agreed I played it well;
The servants bounded when I rang the bell;
I used to feed on immemorial carp.

But now I wander in a pathless fen,
Unkinged, forsook, discredited, discrowned;
I who was born to be the King of Men,
I who made armies tremble when I frowned,

I—in a neat-herd's damp and draughty hut—
Perform the menial duties of a slut.

Do you think the last rhyme weak? (*The* NEAT-HERD *does not answer.*) We have also written a ballad, but we cannot remember all of it. It is addressed to Guthrum, King of the Danes. The *Envoi*, however, runs like this.

Prince, you are having the time of your life,
From the Straits of Dover to Glaston Tor,
And writing it home to your Danish wife;—
But where are the bones and the hammer of Thor?

If we had a harp with us we would sing you the music, but we are sorry to say we lost it in the marsh yesterday.

THE NEAT-HERD. Oo! AR!

Enter the NEAT-HERD'S WIFE

THE NEAT-HERD'S WIFE. Be the baatch ready?

THE KING. Oh yes, of course. We shall be delighted.

[*He hurriedly lifts the tray with the loaves from the hearth and places it on the table.*

THE NEAT-HERD'S WIFE. Drat th' man! If they bain't all burnt! Ye take strange folk to house, and aask un to mind the baatch and turn't, and draat un if they doan't forget to turn when they be burning. Ize warrant ye be ready enough to eat un when they be done! Drat the man if I haven't half a mind to give un a beating with th' rolling-pin! Not a morsel shall ee get; good-for-nothing, idle, vagabond, wastrel, ramscullion, thief, robber.

THE NEAT-HERD. Easy, old woman, ee be th' *King!*

THE NEAT-HERD'S WIFE. Well, and if that bain't like a man, to let me tongue run on not knowing nothing neither! (*Curtsying.*) I'm zure I beg your Majesty's humble pardon, and I'm zure I knew nothing and meant no harm; and my man be that foolish not to tell a body that the King's self be here, so homelike and all, taking pity on us poor folk. I'm zure as I meant no harm, and I do for to beg your Majesty's pardon, and that I do, an' right humbly.

THE KING. Do not mention it. We assure you it is not of the slightest consequence. It was exceedingly careless of us to burn your loaves—your admirably kneaded loaves. And we most humbly and sincerely apologise. We are, we are afraid, given to these fits, these sudden and unwarrantable fits of absent-mindedness.

THE NEAT-HERD'S WIFE. And me always a-wanting to see a real Dane, too! Only yesterday I zaid t' Mary, "Mary," I do zay, "the Danes be all over the country." "Lord-amercy," she zay, "who be they!" "I bain't zet eyes on one on un yet," zay I, "but folks do zay as they be mighty pleasant folk," zav I: and now to have the

King of the Danes himself in my hut. . . . Well, who'd a thought as zuch a thing would coom to me an' mine !

THE NEAT-HERD. Ye be mistaken, ye be. He bain't the Danish King, he be t'other, he that wur th' King of England—bor ! Alfred as was——

THE NEAT-HERD'S WIFE. What?

THE NEAT-HERD. Th' King o' England as was till th' Danes coom ower ! Alfred they called 'un !

THE NEAT-HERD'S WIFE. He as be driven away, like?

THE NEAT-HERD. Oo ! AR !

THE NEAT-HERD'S WIFE (*to the* KING). Oh, you be he, be you? Then ye ought to be ashamed of yoursel', that ye ought, coming into strange folk's houses at this time o' day, and begging for bread; and then when they've pity on ye for your misery, and give ye the chance of turning an honest penny by a piece of work as mony a man'd be glad to get, and any child could ha' done better, forgetting to turn th' loaves and spoiling th' whole baatch; an' ye know well enow I can't baake again this week —not that I mind th' baatch; but I can't have ye here, nohow ! Ye'd best be a-going, and that quick ! Bor !

THE KING. But cannot you possibly let us remain here until to-morrow? We are in need of shelter for the night.

THE NEAT-HERD. Don't be too 'ard on him, old 'ooman.

THE NEAT-HERD'S WIFE. Be ye daaft? We'd ha' the Danish soldiers, th' archers, and th' whole Danish army here in no time for a-sheltering a traitor like, and a rubbul. I reckon we're honest folk, and loyal servants of the King, and we bain't be going to shelter any gurt rubbul here. I'ze brought up to be loyal; I'ze warrant I'm a loyal servant till I do die. No rubbuls here. Out ye go, ye scurvy traitor, and that quick, ye knave, or else I'll bring my rolling-pin to ye! Not that I grudge ye a morsel. There, ye may take one of them burnt cakes with ye, that ye may, and enjoy it, too. And now out with ye, avoor one o' th' neighbours caatch a sight on ye. Out, do ye 'ear me! out!

THE KING (*sighing*). Very well, we are going. (*To himself*) Nothing fails like failure, but perhaps a time will come. (*He goes out peevishly, biting his nails.*)

CURTAIN.

XX

ROSAMUND AND ELEANOR

SCENE.—*A room in* ROSAMUND'S *house, " The Laby-rinth," Woodstock. Discovered :* ROSAMUND (*playing a harp*) *and* MARGERY. *It is night.*

MARGERY. There's a lady wishes to see you, milady.

ROSAMUND. A lady! How can she have found her way through the Labyrinth? You know that I'm not at home to any visitors. (*She throws down her harp.*)

MARGERY. She said she wished to see your ladyship very particular.

ROSAMUND. Who is she?

MARGERY. She didn't give any name, but she said it was something about fortune-telling.

ROSAMUND. Oh ! she's the fortune-teller I heard about—the gipsy.

MARGERY. She's not that sort, milady.

ROSAMUND. Do you mean she's a lady?

MARGERY. She's dressed poor—but——

ROSAMUND. What?

MARGERY. Well, milady, I thought she had come to beg, what with her poor clothes; but when I said as you were not at home to visitors, she ordered me about like, so rough, that I saw at once she was a real lady; and then her shoes are beautiful, I'm sure, the best red velvet.

ROSAMUND (*pensively*). I promised Henry not to see any one—but then once can't matter—and I do so want to have my fortune told. (*Abruptly*) Show her in. (*Exit* MARGERY.) After all, Henry never need know. And I don't see why I should never see a soul. I am becoming quite rusty for want of human society. Besides, Henry promised to let me have my fortune told.

Enter MARGERY *and* QUEEN ELEANOR. QUEEN
    ELEANOR *is a commanding-looking woman, shabbily
    dressed.* MARGERY *withdraws.*

ROSAMUND (*rising shyly*). How do you do?

ELEANOR. Please sit down. I will sit down too. (*They both sit down.*) You have got a beautiful house.

ROSAMUND. Yes, isn't it nice? Mavis built it.

ELEANOR. Mavis! Really? I've always considered him too extravagant for me.

ROSAMUND. You ought to come in the day time and see the garden. The roses are beautiful this year. I beg your pardon, but I didn't quite catch your name.

ELEANOR. Never mind about my name. I've come to talk business. How long have you been living here?

ROSAMUND. Let me see, we—I mean I—go in on Lady Day. But aren't you going to tell my fortune?

ELEANOR. So you do wish your fortune told?

ROSAMUND. Oh yes, please tell it me if you can.

ELEANOR. All in good time.

ROSAMUND. But before you do so, you won't be offended, I'm sure, if I ask you how you found your way through the Labyrinth?

ELEANOR. Fortune-tellers know that kind of thing by instinct.

ROSAMUND (*greatly interested*). Really? Then you must tell me who is going to be champion at the Winchester Tournament, and whether (*she hesitates*)——

ELEANOR. What?

ROSAMUND. Oh! Nothing. How do you tell one's fortune? By looking at the hand or in a crystal?

ELEANOR. I will look at your hand first. Show it me. No; the left hand first, please. (ROSAMUND *gives her her left hand.*) Yours is a most interesting hand. The Mountain of the Moon is strongly developed.

ROSAMUND. Oh! How interesting! What does that mean?

ELEANOR. It means that you have a warm, affectionate nature.

ROSAMUND. That's true.

ELEANOR. You had several illnesses when you were a child.

ROSAMUND. Yes; I had whooping-cough when I was four, measles when I was seven, and scarlatina when I was nine.

ELEANOR. Exactly. You have more intuition than judgment; your first instincts are true, but you are inclined to let them be overruled by your second thoughts.

ROSAMUND. That's perfectly true.

ELEANOR. You are very generous, but inclined to be extravagant in dress. You are fond of luxury, devoted to flowers, and you like soft stuffs. You are fond of music, but you have more taste than actual skill. You are quick-tempered, but not resentful; you are gentle, modest, and unassuming, but inclined to be obstinate, if you are driven beyond a certain point.

ROSAMUND. It's too wonderful!

ELEANOR. The Mountain of Jupiter is highly developed; Saturn fair, and Mercury almost imperceptible. That means you are ambitious but easy-going, rather lazy, and most careless about money matters.

ROSAMUND. It's like second sight.

ELEANOR. You have had one great love affair in your life. (*She pauses.*)

ROSAMUND. Do go on.

ELEANOR. The man you love is tall; he has red hair, almost the colour of a ruby, and a violent temper. He is impulsive, and often does things on the spur of the moment which he regrets bitterly afterwards.

ROSAMUND. Yes, yes.

ELEANOR. He is a powerful man. He holds a position of great importance in the State.

ROSAMUND. And will he love me for ever and ever?

ELEANOR. You have a double line of life, and it is marked with a star.

ROSAMUND. What does that mean?

ELEANOR. It means that the man you love is threatened with a great disaster.

ROSAMUND. Oh! How dreadful! Is there no means by which it can be averted?

ELEANOR. There is one way.

ROSAMUND. What is it? Tell me quickly.

ELEANOR (*solemnly*). By an act of willing self-

sacrifice on your part. That is to say, by your death
—self-inflicted, of course. If you give up your life
you will save your lover's.

ROSAMUND. Oh!

ELEANOR. And you will go down to posterity as
a devoted woman—a heroine.

ROSAMUND. Oh!

ELEANOR. But unless you perform this act of
self-sacrifice at once, it will be too late. The danger
is imminent.

ROSAMUND. What kind of danger is it?

ELEANOR. On that point the stars are reticent.

ROSAMUND. But tell me more about the—about
him.

ELEANOR. About whom?

ROSAMUND. The man with ruby hair. Is he
married?

ELEANOR. Yes, and hence the trouble. He is
married to a high-born, noble, unselfish, generous,
gifted, and beautiful woman—a paragon. But I
am sorry to say, he has for a brief moment proved
faithless to her in thought—it is only a temporary
whim, of course; but even a passing infidelity—
even though it be only an infidelity in thought—is
at once visited with a just retribution. It is because
of the infidelity that he is now meditating, that the
vengeance of the stars pursues him, and that danger
threatens.

ROSAMUND. It's not true! His wife is horrible.
She has driven him away by her cold, callous
conduct. She's a scold. She bullies him. She
nags at him from morning till night. Besides
which she's very, very ugly, and dresses like a
scarecrow.

ELEANOR. How dare you talk like that to me! On your knees, wretched minx!

ROSAMUND. I don't believe you're a fortune-teller at all. I don't believe you know anything about it.

ELEANOR. You are right. I am no fortune-teller. I am the Queen. My name is Eleanor.

ROSAMUND. Oh dear! You've no business to come here. This is my house.

ELEANOR. Your house, indeed! However, I have not come here to waste my time. I have come, as I said before, on business. Here is a dagger, and here in this vial is an effective but entirely painless poison. I give you two minutes to choose which way you will take it.

[*She places the vial and the dagger on a small table.*

ROSAMUND (*crying*). Oh! Go! You frighten me.

ELEANOR. Now, do you hear what I say? Two minutes.

ROSAMUND (*kneeling and sobbing*). I can't. Oh, please spare me! I will do anything; I will go away—anywhere—to a nunnery; but please spare me.

ELEANOR (*with tragic grimness*). One minute and a half.

ROSAMUND. Oh, I'm so young! I'm sure I never meant any harm. Spare my life. Have mercy!

ELEANOR. One minute.

ROSAMUND. Oh, you are cruel. I'm so young. Think what it is to be young.

ELEANOR. The time has elapsed. Now, which is it to be?

ROSAMUND (*rising and drying her eyes*). After all, why should I? (*She takes the dagger and the vial and throws them on to the floor.*) I won't take either. So there! You can do your worst. (*She calls*) Here, Margery! Rosalie! Topaz! Anselm! Richard! Thomas! Quick! Help! Murder! (*Margery and a bevy of servants rush into the room with torches and staves.*) This fortune-teller has insulted me! Turn her out of the house at once!

ELEANOR. How dare you! I'm the——

ROSAMUND. Quick! Quick! Turn her out. She's tried to poison me! If you don't turn her out at once I'll tell the King——

[*The servants turn out* QUEEN ELEANOR, *who struggles violently.*

ROSAMUND. Mind, Margery, if there should be *any* other visitors, I'm not at home.

CURTAIN.

XXI

ARIADNE IN NAXOS

SCENE.—*A room in* ARIADNE'S *house at Naxos.
Discovered:* ARIADNE *and* ŒNONE, *her
attendant.*

ARIADNE. When Theseus comes, show him in
here directly. I am expecting Dionysus in half an
hour. If he comes sooner, which he probably will
do, don't announce him, but show him into the
dining-room, and then come in here and make up
the fire so that I may know he's there. You quite
understand?

ŒNONE. Yes, perfectly.

ARIADNE. There is Theseus walking up the
drive. Go and let him in quickly.

[ŒNONE *goes out.*

[ARIADNE *arranges herself by a spinning-wheel,
near a fire where myrtle-twigs are burning, in
an attitude of simple, brave, and unaffected
dejection. She rubs her eyes with a silken scarf
to make them appear red.*

Enter THESEUS

ARIADNE (*smiling bravely*). It's wonderful of you
to be so punctual.

THESEUS. Yes, I——

ARIADNE. Sit down here. Or do you mind the fire?

THESEUS. No, I assure you.

ARIADNE. Are you quite sure you don't mind the fire?

THESEUS. I like it, really.

ARIADNE. Perhaps you would like a screen?

THESEUS. No, I promise you.

[ARIADNE *rings a small silver hand-bell.* No, please don't ring.

Enter ŒNONE

ARIADNE. You may just as well have the screen. It's there. Œnone, will you please bring a screen for the Duke? The fire's so hot.

[ŒNONE *goes out.*

ARIADNE. Would you like a little wine?

THESEUS. No, thank you, really; I never drink wine in the morning.

ARIADNE. There's some in the next room, if you would like to have some.

Enter ŒNONE, *bringing a screen, which she puts in front of* THESEUS

THESEUS. Oh, thank you so much!

[ŒNONE *goes out.*

ARIADNE. Is that right for you?

THESEUS. That's perfect! (*With nervous decision*) I've come to tell you that I'm so sorry I was rude yesterday, and that of course I didn't mean——

ARIADNE. When you get to Athens I want you to do something for me. Do you think you will have time? Do you think you could possibly remember it? It would be too heroic of you if you would.

THESEUS. Of course I would; but——

ARIADNE. It's the most tiresome commission . . . I want you to send me two pounds of Hymettus honey.

THESEUS. But I really wasn't thinking of——

ARIADNE. Will you have it sent by the next messenger, care of the King, to Crete, and then I shan't have to pay the duty?

THESEUS. But really, Ariadne——

ARIADNE. And you won't forget to give your father a hundred messages from me, will you? I hope they've packed the Minotaur's head properly. It would be a terrible tragedy if the horns were broken.

THESEUS. I haven't had anything packed yet. I really——

ARIADNE. Œnone will help to pack for you. She's a wonderful packer. (*She rings the bell.*) She packs like an angel.

THESEUS. But my slave can do it; besides, I really want——

Enter ŒNONE

ARIADNE. Oh, Œnone, I want you to go round to the Duke's house later—when the doctor comes —and help to pack the Duke's things; and at the same time you might see that the slaves pack the Minotaur's head properly.

ŒNONE. Yes. [*She goes out.*

THESEUS. Ariadne, I must really tell you——

ARIADNE. Let me think : you will get to Athens the day after to-morrow. You won't forget to let me hear what kind of a crossing you have. And you must take warm enough things with you. It's always quite bitter on board that ship. But of course you're a good sailor, aren't you?

THESEUS. I don't mind a long voyage, but sometimes just crossing the isthmus upsets me.

ARIADNE. I have got some wonderful stuff Æsculapius gave me. It's quite harmless. You take one dose two hours before starting and one dose when you get on board; then you lie down; but you must eat nothing. It's wonderful. It's called *Asphodol*. I like the name so much, don't you? You had better have the Minotaur registered straight through to the Piræus. Then you won't have any bother at the other ports with the Customs. If you do have any tiresome bother, you can use my father's name; I will give you the passport he had made out for us. I have scratched my name out, but that will not matter. I have always found them very civil in Greece. They let me bring in bushels of silk from Tyre. You must give my love to Hippolyta, if you see her. She's not been well lately.

THESEUS. Really?

ARIADNE. No, poor darling! I've been rather worried and anxious about her. She's been having that horrible neuritis again. I had a letter yesterday from Athens, saying that she had lost her buoyancy and had had to give up riding altogether! Isn't it too terrible? She was such an inspired rider, wasn't she, with those hands and that unerring judgment? I can't imagine anything more ironical and more tragic; and they say she's so brave about it. She would be, of course. Don't you think people like that always surprise one by being a little better than their best in an emergency?

THESEUS. Yes.

ARIADNE. Don't you think Hippolyta is the most straight and true character we have ever known?

THESEUS (*uncomfortable*). Yes, yes——

ARIADNE. And almost more beautiful than anybody?

THESEUS. Yes, she is beautiful.

ARIADNE. I love her straightness of line, and her strong capable hands, and that *magic* cast in her left eye, which gives a kind of strangeness to her face, doesn't it?

THESEUS. She is very good-looking.

ARIADNE. But don't you think much more than that? Don't you put her almost higher than anybody for charm?

THESEUS. I'd never thought about her like that.

ARIADNE. And then isn't she quite unlike any one else? Doesn't one feel absolutely certain with her, like one does with a perfect chariot-driver?

THESEUS. Yes, she has a very fine character.

ARIADNE. Almost more than fine, isn't it? Something rare?

THESEUS. But, Ariadne, I really must——

ARIADNE. You needn't go yet. You've lots of time to pack. Œnone will help with the packing. You don't sail till sunset, do you? Because of the tide. I hope you've got the right pilot. The old man with one eye. He's too charming. He's my greatest friend.

THESEUS. Ariadne——

ARIADNE. I shall watch you from the hill. I shan't come down to the quay because of the crowd —you might wave from the ship. You will be able to see me. I shall stand next to the clump of cypress-trees and watch the ship till she's out of sight. There's a new moon to-night, just as there was the first night you arrived at Crete. Do you remember how papa bored you by talking about astrology? And you were so angelically kind to him and patient. You bore it so well. It was like you. I don't think you know how devoted papa is to you, and how much he will miss you.

THESEUS. Ariadne—please——

ARIADNE. You won't forget to write and say whether the Minotaur arrives safely, will you? Because papa will simply be longing to know, and he'd be miserable if anything went wrong.

THESEUS (*getting up and knocking down the screen in his agitation*). Ariadne, I simply can't bear this any longer. I must speak. You must and shall hear me. The whole thing's a mistake—a nightmare. I swear I didn't mean a thing yesterday. It was too stupid of me to—to say—I mean I didn't mean—I mean I lost my temper—just like any one. Of course I didn't mean, really.

Enter ŒNONE. *She brings in a large bundle of fire-wood, which she throws on to the hearth*

ARIADNE (*getting up*). I'm afraid you oughtn't to stay another minute now, or else you will miss the ship—Œnone will go with you and help you to pack. Good-bye, Theseus. It's been too perfect, hasn't it? I have loved it all so. You won't forget the honey, will you? Two pounds. Now you'll really have to run—and I have got the doctor coming in one second. Good-bye, Theseus, and my best love to your father and to dear Hippolyta if you see her. Œnone, please go with the Duke.

[ARIADNE *shakes hands with* THESEUS.

THESEUS. But, really——

ARIADNE. I'm afraid I must fly. I hope you'll have a perfect crossing.

THESEUS (*hopelessly*). Good-bye, Ariadne——

[*He goes out very sadly with* ŒNONE *L. As soon as they are gone,* ARIADNE *gently opens a door R. and calls :* Dionysus !

Enter DIONYSUS

DIONYSUS. Has he gone?

ARIADNE. Yes, at last, I think. Haven't I managed it too beautifully? He was longing not to go away at all.

DIONYSUS. When does he sail?

ARIADNE. At sunset. Sit down. We've got millions of things to say, haven't we? Do you mind the fire? There's the screen there on the floor—if you do——

DIONYSUS. No, I love it.

CURTAIN.

XXII

VELASQUEZ AND THE "VENUS"

SCENE.—VELASQUEZ'S *studio.* DONA SOL, *a beautiful dark-haired lady, elaborately dressed in stiff
farthingale, is sitting for her portrait.* VELAS-
QUEZ *is standing in front of an easel, vehemently
throwing paint on to the canvas with a large, long
brush. In the corner of the studio is an open
virginal.*

VELASQUEZ. Are you getting tired?

DONA SOL. No, I never get tired of sitting; I'm
so used to standing up at Court.

VELASQUEZ. Would you mind turning your head
a shade to the left? Yes, that's right.

DONA SOL. You will be careful about the nose,
won't you?

VELASQUEZ. Ah! you've a very wonderful nose
from the painter's point of view.

DONA SOL. They always exaggerate my nose—
and I do so hate exaggeration, don't you?

VELASQUEZ (*absently*). Yes.

DONA SOL. Shall I be able to see the picture
to-day?

VELASQUEZ. I think so. It's practically finished
now. I have only got to finish that piece of lace on
your left wrist.

DONA SOL. Shan't you want another sitting?

VELASQUEZ. No—I——

DONA SOL. But Dona Anna had a dozen sittings.

VELASQUEZ. But she's fair—I find fair people more difficult to paint.

DONA SOL. I can't see what there was to paint in her at all. She's all bones.

VELASQUEZ. That's just it. I can't get that lace right. Do you mind if I play a tune on the virginal?

DONA SOL. No, please do.

[VELASQUEZ *goes to the virginal and plays a wild, rhythmic dance.*

DONA SOL. Is that Moorish?

VELASQUEZ. No. English. Quaint, isn't it? It's what they call a Morris-dance. Isn't it charming?

DONA SOL. Yes. I love English music. It's so uncivilised and fresh.

VELASQUEZ. Yes, they are a wonderfully musical people. (*He breaks off in the middle of the tune.*) I've got it. (*He runs to the canvas and flings a piece of white paint on to it.*) Ah, that's it. It's finished.

DONA SOL. What, the whole picture?

VELASQUEZ (*with a sigh of relief*). Yes, the whole picture.

DONA SOL. May I look?

VELASQUEZ. Certainly.

[DONA SOL *gets down from the platform and walks to the easel.*

DONA SOL. It's wonderful, Velasquez; quite wonderful. I like it enormously. You haven't quite finished the hands yet, have you?

VELASQUEZ. Yes, I think the hands will do like that. You don't quite get the light where you're standing. If you come here you'll see better.

DONA SOL (*moving*). I think its wonderful. Only I should like the hands to be a little more distinct. The dress is beautiful, and so is the necklace. But you've made my blue ribbon look green.

VELASQUEZ. That's the sun on it.

DONA SOL. But it isn't green. It's blue. Look at it. No amount of sun will make this blue into green.

VELASQUEZ. You see, the sun was full on it yesterday.

DONA SOL. I think it's all perfect, except the nose. My nose is tip-tilted, and you've given me a nose like a potato. You *must* alter that. I know my nose is difficult.

VELASQUEZ (*slightly darkening a shadow on the face*). Is that better?

DONA SOL. Yes, that's better. But it's still a little too heavy. You see, my nose is my best feature. I don't mind what you do to my hair and my mouth. I don't want to criticise. I never do criticise my own portraits. In fact, I think it's quite absurd for the sitter to criticise a picture. But I do think I'm a rather good judge of noses. Couldn't you make it just a shade more delicate?

VELASQUEZ (*giving the nose a touch with the brush.*) Is that better?

DONA SOL. Yes, that's better. I think that really is better. (*A pause.*) Don't you think you could make the eyebrows a little darker? You've made them so faint. And then I think the hair ought to be a little brighter, and the expression a shade less severe. I don't think you've quite got my smile. I look cross. Of course I suppose I look like that sometimes—when everything goes wrong. Every one does look cross sometimes—but that's not what I usually look like.

VELASQUEZ (*making a few imperceptible alterations*). Is that better?

DONA SOL. Yes, that's much better. I think it's perfect. May I look at some of the other pictures?

[*She walks round the studio till she finds several canvases turned face backwards against a heavy piece of furniture.*

VELASQUEZ. Let me help you. (*He turns several pictures round.*)

DONA SOL. Ah, that's the King. It's quite excellent. And that's the dear old Admiral. It's exactly like him. Oh, and that's Dona Elvira— *how* like, but *how* cruel!—How could you do that? Didn't she mind dreadfully? And what a dear little girl! That's not finished, I suppose? Oh, and I do love that seapiece. It's a storm, I suppose?

VELASQUEZ. I'm afraid it's meant to be a man riding in a field. It's just a study.

DONA SOL. Of course it is. How stupid of me. I couldn't see properly. It's wonderful—quite wonderful. And what's that large picture on an easel over there with a curtain over it?

VELASQUEZ. Oh, that's nothing. It's only a sketch—it's not finished.

DONA SOL. Do let me see it.

VELASQUEZ. I'm afraid I can't, really.

DONA SOL. But I insist on seeing it. I've been such a good sitter. Now I'm going to pull the curtain off.

VELASQUEZ. It's not my picture at all. It's not by me. It's by one of my pupils. It's by Mazo.

DONA SOL. Then of course I can see it. (*She pulls away the curtain, revealing a picture of Venus looking into a glass.*) Oh, but that's my head! How dared you do such a thing? No wonder you didn't want me to see it. Oh, how could you do such a thing?

VELASQUEZ. But I assure you you're mistaken. In the first place, I never painted the picture. I never touched it. It's Mazo's work. And he did it out of his head. At least, he did it from a model. It's meant to be Eros and Psyche or Venus, I've forgotten which.

DONA SOL. How could you put my head on such a hideous body? I call it mean, odious, and cowardly, and quite unpardonable. I shall burn my picture.

VELASQUEZ. But, my dear lady, do listen to me for one moment. The picture's not my work. I flatter myself really that I can draw a little better than that. That's mere apprentice work. Just compare it with my pictures. I never use those hot reds and those dull, lifeless greys. Just compare it with the other pictures.

DONA SOL (*crying*). How can I compare it with the others? You've never dared paint any one else like that.

VELASQUEZ. And then the face in the glass is no more your face than it is mine. It's not the least

like you. It's a model's face. Mazo may have got
a hint, a suggestion, quite unconsciously from seeing
my picture, but nothing more. He's never set eyes
on you.

DONA SOL. I don't believe it's by Mazo. I believe
it's by you—or else you wouldn't have been so anxious
for me not to see it.

VELASQUEZ. Well, I promise you that Mazo
painted that picture from a model—a flower girl.
I saw him do it. But to satisfy you, he shall get
another model and paint in a different face.

DONA SOL. That's the least you can do.

VELASQUEZ. It shall be done to-day. Mazo's
coming here this morning.

DONA SOL. Will you promise me that the face
will be *quite, quite* different?

VELASQUEZ. On my word of honour as a Spaniard
and as a painter.

DONA SOL (*drying her eyes*). Very well, I will forgive you—on one condition.

VELASQUEZ. What is it?

DONA SOL. That you will change the nose in *my*
picture and make it less like a potato.

VELASQUEZ. Of course I will.

DONA SOL. Very well then. Good-bye. I shall
come back to-morrow morning and see,—but oh!
what a shame!

[VELASQUEZ *makes a low bow and leads her out.*
He comes back and, opening a door into a room
adjoining the studio, he calls : Mazo!

Enter MAZO

VELASQUEZ. The "Venus" is by you. Do you

hear me? You painted it. And you must change the face.

MAZO. I don't understand—change it in what way?

VELASQUEZ. You must change it altogether. Paint in any face you like. And you must say you painted the whole picture. Do it at once, and put your signature somewhere in the picture too.

MAZO. But, master, it's one of your greatest triumphs.

VELASQUEZ. I know that as well as you do— nevertheless, that picture must go to the King and be known to all the world as a Mazo, and not as a Velasquez.

CURTAIN.

XXIII

XANTIPPE AND SOCRATES

Scene.—*A room in* Socrates' *house.* Xantippe *is seated at a table, on which an unappetising meal, consisting of figs, parsley, and some hashed goat's meat, is spread.*

Enter Socrates

Xantippe. You're twenty minutes late.

Socrates. I'm sorry, I was kept——

Xantippe. Wasting your time as usual, I suppose, and bothering people with questions who have got something better to do than to listen to you. You can't think what a mistake you make by going on like that. You can't think how much people dislike it. If people enjoyed it, or admired it, I could understand the waste of time—but they don't. It only makes them angry. Everybody's saying so.

Socrates. Who's everybody?

Xantippe. There you are with your questions again. Please don't try to catch me out with those kind of tricks. I'm not a philosopher. I'm not a sophist. I know I'm not clever—I'm only a woman. But I do know the difference between right and wrong and black and white, and I don't 'hink it's very kind of you, or very generous either, to be always pointing out my ignorance, and perpetually making me the butt of your sarcasm.

SOCRATES. But I never said a word.

XANTIPPE. Oh, please, don't try to wriggle out of it. We all know you're very good at that. I do hate that shuffling so. It's so cowardly. I do like a man one can trust—and depend on—who when he says Yes means Yes, and when he says No means No.

SOCRATES. I'm sorry I spoke.

XANTIPPE. I suppose that's what's called irony. I've no doubt it's very clever, but I'm afraid it's wasted on me. I should keep those remarks for the market-place and the gymnasia and the workshops. I've no doubt they'd be highly appreciated there by that clique of young men who do nothing but admire each other. I'm afraid I'm old-fashioned. I was brought up to think a man should treat his wife with decent civility, and try, even if he did think her stupid, not to be always showing it.

SOCRATES. Have I by a word or hint ever suggested that you were stupid?

XANTIPPE. Oh, of course not—never. However, we won't discuss that. We will change the subject, if you don't mind.

SOCRATES. But really——

XANTIPPE (*ignoring the interruption*). Please give me your plate. I will help you to the goat.

SOCRATES. None for me, thank you, to-day.

XANTIPPE. Why not? I suppose it's not good enough. I'm afraid I can't provide the food you get at your grand friends' houses, but I do think it's rather cruel of you to sneer at my poor humble efforts.

SOCRATES. I promise you, Xantippe, nothing was farther from my thoughts. I'm not hungry. I've really got no appetite for meat to-day. I'll have some figs, if you don't mind.

XANTIPPE. I suppose that's a new fad, not to eat meat. I assure you people talk quite enough about you as it is without your making yourself more peculiar. Only yesterday Chrysilla was talking about your clothes. She asked if you made them dirty on purpose. She said the spots on the back couldn't have got there by accident. Every one notices it—every one says the same thing. Of course they think it's my fault. No doubt it's very amusing for people who don't mind attracting attention and who like being notorious; but it *is* rather hard on me. And when I hear people saying " Poor Socrates ! it is such a shame that his wife looks after him so badly and doesn't even mend his sandals "—I admit I do feel rather hurt. However, that would never enter into your head. A philosopher hasn't time to think of other people. I suppose unselfishness doesn't form part of a sophist's training, does it?

[SOCRATES *says nothing, but eats first one fig and then another.*

XANTIPPE. I think you might at least answer when you're spoken to. I am far from expecting you to treat me with consideration or respect; but I do expect ordinary civility.

[SOCRATES *goes on eating figs in silence.*

XANTIPPE. Oh, I see, you're going to sulk. First you browbeat, then you're satirical. Then you sneer at the food, and then you sulk.

SOCRATES. I never said a word against the food.

XANTIPPE. You never said a word against the food. You only kept me waiting nearly half an hour for dinner—not that that was anything new —I'm sure I ought to be used to that by now—and you only refused to look at the dish which I had taken pains to cook with my own hands for you.

SOCRATES. All I said was I wasn't hungry—that I had no appetite for meat.

XANTIPPE. You've eaten all the figs. You've got quite an appetite for those.

SOCRATES. That's different.

XANTIPPE. Oh, that's different, is it? One can be hungry enough to eat all the fruit there is in the house, which I was especially keeping for this evening, but not hungry enough to touch a piece of meat. I suppose that's algebra.

SOCRATES. You know I very rarely eat meat.

XANTIPPE. Really? I hadn't noticed it. I always hear of your eating meat in other people's houses; but my poor cooking is not good enough for you. I'm sorry, but I can't afford those spicy, messy dishes. If I had a husband who had a *real* profession, and worked, and did something useful to earn his living and support his house and home, it would be different; only I think the least you could do is not to sneer at one when one is only trying to do one's best.

SOCRATES. I very rarely eat meat anywhere now.

XANTIPPE. That's why you're looking so ill. All the doctors say it's a mistake. Some people can do without meat They don't need it—but a man who works with his brain like you do *ought* to eat nourishing food. You ought to force yourself to eat meat, even if you don't feel inclined to.

SOCRATES. I thought you said just now that I did nothing.

XANTIPPE. There you are, cross-examining me like a lawyer, and tripping me up. I've no doubt it's very amusing for a professional philosopher to catch out a poor ignorant woman like me. It's a pity your audience isn't here. They *would* enjoy it. However, I'm afraid I'm not impressed. You can twist my words into anything you like. You can prove I meant black when I said white, but you know perfectly well what I mean. You know as well as I do that your eccentricity has made you thoroughly unpopular. And what I say is, it's just these little things that matter. Now do put all that nonsense away and have some goat.

SOCRATES. No, thank you. I really can't.

XANTIPPE. It's excellent goat, and there's some garlic in the sauce. I hate garlic, and it's there on purpose for you——

SOCRATES. Oh !

XANTIPPE. Give me your plate.

SOCRATES. I'd really rather not.

XANTIPPE. It would do you all the good in the world.

SOCRATES. But I've had quite enough. I've finished.

XANTIPPE. I suppose you had dinner before you came here, or you're going to have dinner somewhere else presently.

SOCRATES. I haven't touched food since I left the house.

XANTIPPE. Then it's quite ridiculous your not eating. Let me give you some goat at once.

SOCRATES. I couldn't, really. Besides, I must go in a minute.

XANTIPPE. There! I knew it! You're going out to dinner.

SOCRATES. You are mistaken, Xantippe.

XANTIPPE. You'd far better tell me the truth at once. I'm quite certain to find it out sooner or later. You can't think how foolish it is to tell lies and then be found out afterwards. You can't think how much a woman despises a man for that—you couldn't do anything more foolish.

SOCRATES. I promise you by all the gods that I'm not going to dine elsewhere.

XANTIPPE. I suppose you don't expect me to fall into that trap! Swearing by all the gods, when every one in Athens knows you are a professed atheist —when you do nothing but mock the gods from morning till night—and, what's far worse, make other people mock them too; when I scarcely like to have a slave in the house because of your impiety—and your blasphemy.

SOCRATES. I really think you are rather unfair, Xantippe. You will be sorry for this some day.

XANTIPPE. Then may I ask where you are going?

SOCRATES. I've got an important engagement.

XANTIPPE. And with whom?

SOCRATES. I would rather not say, for your sake.

XANTIPPE. That's very clever and ingenious to put it on me. But I'm tired of being bullied. Even a worm will turn, and I demand to be treated just for once like a human being, and with the minimum of courtesy and frankness. I don't ask for your confidence, I know that would be useless. But I do ask to be treated with a grain of straightforwardness and honesty. I insist upon it. I have borne your sneers, your sarcasm, and your sulkiness, your irritability, your withering silence, quite long enough. I will not put up with it any longer.

SOCRATES. Very well. Since you will have it, I have been impeached by Lycon, Meletus, and Anytus on some ridiculous charge, the result of which, however, may be extremely serious—in fact it may be a matter of life or death—and I am obliged to appear before them at once.

XANTIPPE. Oh dear, oh dear! I always said so. I knew it would come to this! This is what comes of not eating meat like a decent citizen!

[XANTIPPE *bursts into tears.*

CURTAIN.

XXIV

CALYPSO

First performed by Officers of H.M.S. Calypso at Gibraltar, March 1928; performed at the Adelphi Theatre, May 6th 1928.

SCENE.—*A Grotto in the Island of Ogygia.* CALYPSO *discovered, looking languid. Enter* STEWARD.

STEWARD.   There is *one* god outside for you.

CALYPSO.   One what ?

STEWARD.   One god from Olympus.

CALYPSO.   Which one ?

STEWARD.   One very nice god with wings on his feet.

CALYPSO.   It's Mercury. Show him in.

   [CALYPSO *arranges her face and hair with a hand mirror and lip-stick.*

        Enter STEWARD *and* MERCURY.

MERCURY.   Calypso !

CALYPSO.   Mercury ! Well, this is a surprise !

MERCURY.   I haven't seen you for ages.

CALYPSO.   Not for two centuries. How did you some ?

MERCURY.   I flew.

CALYPSO.   Of course. . . . A drop of nectar ?

MERCURY.   No, no, thank you ; it's much too early.

184

CALYPSO (*through the curtain*). Steward! Two Calypso's. No, two Circe's. (*To* MERCURY.) Well, what's the news?

Enter STEWARD *with two cups. He gives one to* CALYPSO *and one to* MERCURY.

MERCURY. Happy days!

CALYPSO (*wearily*). Happy centuries.

[*They drink.*

MERCURY (*dazed*). That's good. (*He wipes his forehead.*) *Very* good. What is it made of?

CALYPSO. Only honey, mint, juniper, and a dash of wormwood. My sister Circe invented it. I like it because it's not too strong.

MERCURY. No.

Whenever I drink with you, Calypso,

I feel that I might grow to be a dypso.

CALYPSO (*looking at* MERCURY *with satisfaction*). Steward, bring the god an olive.

Enter STEWARD *with snacks on a tray.*
MERCURY *eats an olive.*

You have only drunk half of it.

MERCURY (*recovering control and smiling in triumph at her*). Don't be silly! (*Quite sober and businesslike.*) By the way, isn't Ulysses staying here?

CALYPSO. Yes. He's asleep. He sleeps a great deal. It's the sea air.

MERCURY. Of course, let me see, how long has he been here? Seven years, isn't it?

CALYPSO. No, not quite seven. Six and a half.

MERCURY. Don't you think it's time——

CALYPSO. He went home? I do indeed. Every

day for the last six and a half years I've said to him : You know, Ulysses, I love having you here, but I do think you ought to go home. After all, you are a married man, and I shouldn't like to vex darling Penelope; she must be getting anxious—but he won't hear of going.

MERCURY. Well, they are rather worried about it at Olympus. In fact I have been sent by Jupiter to beg you to let him go.

CALYPSO. *Let* him go ! As if I wanted him to stay ! He's always drunk before dinner, and after dinner he goes to sleep. And then he's a bore—a Trojan War bore. He's beginning to believe it all really happened. I'm longing for him to go, but——

MERCURY. What ?

CALYPSO. How could I send him home without a boat ? You know, I've asked for a boat for centuries.

MERCURY. What about the *Argo ?*

CALYPSO. They won't let her be used.

MERCURY. Economy ?

CALYPSO. Yes. And considering what Venus spends on clothes——

MERCURY (*pensively*). Clothes ?

CALYPSO. My dear Mercury, you know perfectly well there's nothing so costly as simplicity. Golden hair is very expensive, and even leaves——

MERCURY. Yes. Couldn't Ulysses make a raft ?

CALYPSO. What with ?

MERCURY. The pine trees round this grotto.

CALYPSO. What ! Cut down the trees in my garden—the only trees in the island ? Never !

MERCURY. I'd willingly give him a passage, but I'm not allowed to carry mortals.

CALYPSO. Well, you see it's impossible. Please tell Jupiter, with my compliments, that I'm very, very sorry, but it's impossible.

MERCURY. It's no good, Calypso. You've got to let him go. It's an order.

CALYPSO. Very well. But I call it murder, with these currents, and the sea infested with Sirens. Of course, if they want him to be drowned——

MERCURY. Shall I tell him ?

CALYPSO. No, I will. Goddesses understand these things better than gods.

MERCURY. Very well. I must take advantage of the visibility. Good-bye, Calypso. I'm sure to be looking in again soon.

CALYPSO. Good-bye, Mercury. Remember me to all of them.

MERCURY. Good-bye. I'm sure to be looking in again soon.

> [*Exit* MERCURY. *He leaves his winged cap behind him on the floor.*

Steward ! Show the god out, and ask Ulysses to speak to me, if he is up.

> [*Exeunt* STEWARD *and* MERCURY. CALYPSO *pulls down her hair, tears her clothes, and sits on the floor weeping.*
> *Enter* ULYSSES, *looking sleepy and tired.*

ULYSSES (*wearily*). What's the matter now, darling ?

CALYPSO. You're leaving me !

ULYSSES. What on earth put that into your little nead, your lovely little head ?

CALYPSO. Nobody. But I thought by what you said last night that you wanted to go.

ULYSSES. Nonsense !

CALYPSO. Then you don't want to go ?

ULYSSES. Of course not.   How *could* I ?

CALYPSO. And nothing would make you go ?

ULYSSES. Nothing in the whole world.

[*He walks up and down in agitation.*

I swear by all the gods (*he trips up over* MERCURY'S *flying cap.*) What's this ? (*He picks it up.*) A winged cap ?   Has Mercury been here ?

CALYPSO. He did just look in.

ULYSSES. With a message ?

CALYPSO. Nothing of importance.   He was flying over the island, and he landed here to oil his sandals.

ULYSSES. Did he mention me ?

CALYPSO. Yes, he said that they thought at Olympus that you were perhaps fretting to get home, but I told him that we were *very, very* happy.

ULYSSES. I see.

CALYPSO. And then I said that even if you did want to go, there was the boat difficulty.

ULYSSES. Oh, that's no difficulty.   I could easily make a raft.   I prefer small ships to large ones.   I served in rafts for years.

CALYPSO. Then you do want to go ?

ULYSSES. No, I don't *want* to go, but of course an order is an order.

CALYPSO. Who said it was an order ?

ULYSSES. I thought you said that Mercury brought an order from Olympus.   He certainly didn't come here for nothing.   He never flies unless he can help it.   It makes him sick.

CALYPSO. But they can't make you go if you don't want to——

ULYSSES. I shouldn't like you to incur the wrath of Jove.

CALYPSO. Don't bother about me, please.

ULYSSES. And the Grotto isn't thunderbolt-proof.

CALYPSO. I don't mind thunderbolts.

ULYSSES. But I do. I'm not immortal.

CALYPSO. But if you marry me, you will be immortal.

ULYSSES. Mixed marriages are always a mistake. And then, there's Penelope.

CALYPSO. I see. You're going.

ULYSSES. Of course, if it hadn't been an order——

CALYPSO. It wasn't an order, darling. I was only joking. Mercury never even mentioned you. Let's forget all about it.

ULYSSES (*intensely disappointed*). Very well, darling, let's forget all about it.

[*A pause.* ULYSSES *sits looking gloomily in front of him.*

CALYPSO. Will you have a Calypso, darling?

ULYSSES. Yes, please, a Circe. A double one.

Enter MERCURY.

MERCURY. I'm sorry, Calypso, but I think I left my flying cap behind.

CALYPSO. Yes, there it is.

MERCURY. Thank you. Good morning, Ulysses. I suppose Calypso gave you my message?

ULYSSES. No.

MERCURY. You are to proceed forthwith to Ithaca, reporting to the swineherd on arrival. You must find your own transport. They can't give you a boat.

You had better make a raft. A raft is far the safest craft in these waters.

ULYSSES (*joyfully*). Far the safest. The only craft.

MERCURY. Very well. That's understood. I must go at once. It's blowing up. So long, Calypso. (*To* ULYSSES, *smiling and half aside.*) Good luck!

CALYPSO. Mercury always lets one down.

CURTAIN.

XXV

THREE MINUTES

OR

THE DEATH OF CÆSAR*

SCENE I

The stage is divided into three sections. L. CLEOPATRA is lying on a couch. Centre is a telephone exchange in which a female operator is seated, wearing head-pieces, facing the stage and reading the poems of Ovid. R. CÆSAR in his study at a table. Night.

CÆSAR (*taking off a receiver from a telephone*). Tibur, fifty-fifty. No, not Tiger, Tibur. (*Spelling.* T-I-B-U-R. T for Toga, I for Ida, Princess Ida, B) for Balbus, U for Urbs—no, not 'Erb—*Urbs*, R for Rex.
The bell rings

CLEOPATRA. Hullo, who is that, please?

CÆSAR. Is that you, Cleopatra?

CLEOPATRA. Yes, is that you, Cæsar?

CÆSAR. Yes, it's me, Cæsar.

CLEOPATRA. Well?

CÆSAR. I've just been dining with Lepidus..

CLEOPATRA. Yes.

CÆSAR. They want me to go to the Senate to-morrow morning.

CLEOPATRA. Yes.

* At the time of Cæsar's death Cleopatra was living in Rome and fled the country as soon as he was killed.

191

CÆSAR.   To arrange about the campaign.

CLEOPATRA.   Yes.

CÆSAR.   And they say I shall be offered the Crown.

CLEOPATRA.   What, again?

CÆSAR.   Yes, again.

CLEOPATRA.   By Mark Antony?

CÆSAR.   No, by the whole Senate.

CLEOPATRA.   And you will refuse it again.

CÆSAR.   I wanted to refuse it but they want me *not* to.

CLEOPATRA.   Of course they do.

CÆSAR.   Why?

CLEOPATRA.   They know it would be fatal for you to take the title of King. You are quite unpopular enough as it is.

CÆSAR.   I can't see why it should make very much difference.

CLEOPATRA.   It would make *all* the difference.

CÆSAR.   Well, I told them I would accept.

CLEOPATRA.   You must tell them you've changed your mind.

CÆSAR.   It's too late to let them know now.

CLEOPATRA.   You can just *not* go.

CÆSAR.   To the Senate?

CLEOPATRA.   Yes.

CÆSAR.   I must. It's important.

CLEOPATRA.   You can put off going till the day after to-morrow and that will give you time to think it over.

CÆSAR.   I don't like going back on my word.

CLEOPATRA.   You want to be called King.

CÆSAR.   I don't but the people want it.

CLEOPATRA.   I wonder. Who would be Queen?

CÆSAR.   Calpurnia, of course.

CLEOPATRA.   Would she be called Queen?

CÆSAR.   Not Queen regnant—Queen consort.

CLEOPATRA. It sounds too ridiculous, doesn't it ?
Poor Calpurnia ! You wouldn't inflict that on her ?
Have you told her ?

CÆSAR. Not yet.

CLEOPATRA. I shouldn't.

CÆSAR. On the contrary, I mean to tell her at once.
I'm sure she'll agree with me.

CLEOPATRA. I'm sure she won't. She's far too
sensible. She won't want to look ridiculous and to
make you look ridiculous.

CÆSAR. Why should it be ridiculous ?

CLEOPATRA. Anyone in the world will tell you that
to be called Cæsar is dignified, but to be called King
Cæsar is silly. It sounds like the name of a pet dog.

CÆSAR. People will soon get used to it.

CLEOPATRA. Then you are quite determined.

CÆSAR. On what ?

CLEOPATRA. To go to the Senate to-morrow.

CÆSAR. Quite.

CLEOPATRA. And to accept the Crown ?

CÆSAR. Yes.

CLEOPATRA. Why not put it off twenty-four hours ?

CÆSAR. Because when I make up my mind I make
it up. . . .

CLEOPATRA. King Cæsar and Queen Calpurnia !
My poor child ! Really !

CÆSAR. Well, it's going to be !

CLEOPATRA. I know the real reason.

CÆSAR. What ?

CLEOPATRA. You want to wear a crown to hide your
baldness. That laurel wreath you wear doesn't hide it
enough.

TELEPHONE OPERATOR. Three minutes.

CÆSAR *rings off*

SCENE II

The same.   Morning.

CÆSAR.   Tibur, fifty-fifty.

CLEOPATRA (*sleepily*).   Hullo.

CÆSAR.   Is that you, Cleopatra?

CLEOPATRA (*only half-awake*).   Yes, but I've only just been called.   Well, what's your day?

CÆSAR.   It's very cold.

CLEOPATRA (*sleepily*).   I couldn't sleep a wink.   What *is* your day?   Oh! I remember. Are you just starting?

CÆSAR.   What for?

CLEOPATRA.   The Senate.

CÆSAR.   Well, as a matter of fact I'm not sure I'm going to the Senate.

CLEOPATRA.   Oh! really!   Why not?

CÆSAR.   Calpurnia is rather upset.

CLEOPATRA.   Why?

CÆSAR.   Well, she had a bad night.

CLEOPATRA.   Of course she did with that thunderstorm.   We all had bad nights.   My shutters were blown off the wall. . . .

CÆSAR.   Yes, but it was not only that.   Her maid said a lioness had whelped in the yard.

CLEOPATRA.   Why shouldn't it?

CÆSAR.   It's said to be unlucky.   I, of course, am not superstitious.   But the slaves saw ghosts walking about the streets and signs in the sky.

CLEOPATRA.   It was just the storm.

CÆSAR.   Well, just to pacify Calpurnia, I made the priests do sacrifice at once.   The augurers have just sent in their report and they say I had better stay at home to-day as they couldn't find a heart in the beast.

CLEOPATRA.   What sort of beast?

CÆSAR. I don't know. Just an ordinary beast.

CLEOPATRA. The augurers are idiotic. I call that silly.

CÆSAR. It *is* silly, but after all if Calpurnia is nervous—and she is nervous—and begs me not to go to the Senate to-day, the least thing I can do is to put off going till to-morrow.

CLEOPATRA. You are very careful to respect *her* feelings.

CÆSAR. I try to be. She is my wife, after all.

CLEOPATRA. Yes . . . after all. But I think it's silly all the same.

CÆSAR. What ?

CLEOPATRA. Not to go to the Senate.

CÆSAR. Why ?

CLEOPATRA. They'll think you are afraid.

CÆSAR. Of omens ? Ha ! Ha ! they can if they like. I can rise above that.

CLEOPATRA. They'll think it all the same.

CÆSAR. You think I ought to go ?

CLEOPATRA. Yes, of course I do.

CÆSAR. Well, I don't.

CLEOPATRA. I've no doubt you know best.

CÆSAR. I think in this case I *do* know best.

CLEOPATRA. Perhaps it is better you should do as Calpurnia tells you.

CÆSAR. That's nothing to do with it. It's silly to talk like that. I wasn't going anyhow. You persuaded me not to last night.

CLEOPATRA. I did ?

CÆSAR. Yes, you, of course.

CLEOPATRA. I persuaded you not to go to the Senate ?

CÆSAR. You said it would be ridiculous for me to accept the Crown.

CLEOPATRA. Really, Cæsar, may the gods forgive

you ! I never said any such thing ! I said it would be ridiculous for a Queen to be called Queen Consort, that's all. I was in favour of your being King and I am all for your going to the Senate to-day because if you go to-day they will offer you the Crown, but if you put it off till to-morrow, who knows ?

CÆSAR. I have quite made up my mind to refuse it. I hate the sight of a crown.

CLEOPATRA. Well, I think it's very childish not to go to the Senate.

CÆSAR. Possibly I'm childish, but I've made up my mind.

CLEOPATRA. Not to go ?

CÆSAR. Yes ; once my mind's made up it's made up.

CLEOPATRA. Oh, very well.

CÆSAR. Shall I see you to-night ?

CLEOPATRA. I'm afraid not. I've got Mark Antony dining with me.

CÆSAR. But. . . .

OPERATOR. Three minutes.

CLEOPATRA rings off

SCENE III

The same as before. A little later.

CLEOPATRA (*taking off the receiver*). Palatine, one four. No, not Palestine, Palatine. P for Pons, A for Asinorum, L for Lesbia, A for Aspasia, I for idiot, N for Numa, E for Egypt.

CÆSAR. Hullo.

CLEOPATRA. Is that you, Cæsar ?

CÆSAR. Yes, it's me, but I haven't a moment to spare. It's eight o'clock and I am late already.

CLEOPATRA. What have you settled?

CÆSAR. What about?

CLEOPATRA. About going to the Senate.

CÆSAR. Well, I thought over what you said and I came to the conclusion you are right and I *am* going after all.

CLEOPATRA. But, Cæsar, I particularly told you I thought it was a mistake.

CÆSAR. What?

CLEOPATRA. To go to the Senate to-day.

CÆSAR. You really have a very short memory.

CLEOPATRA. And you have no memory at all. I implored you to put it off for twenty-four hours.

CÆSAR. That was last night.

CLEOPATRA. What does it matter *when* it was? I beg you to put it off now.

CÆSAR. It's too late.

CLEOPATRA. Why?

CÆSAR. They are all downstairs waiting for me at this moment in the hall.

CLEOPATRA. Who?

CÆSAR. Brutus and Cassius and the lot. And between you and me, only you mustn't repeat it yet, they *are* going to offer me the Crown *to-day*.

CLEOPATRA. And you?

CÆSAR. I shall refuse it to-day and then see. Wait and see. That is my motto. I came. I waited. I saw.

CLEOPATRA. I ask you as a special favour *not* to go to the Senate to-day.

CÆSAR. Why?

CLEOPATRA. Because I asked my maid the date and she said it was the Ides of March and we were both told to beware of that date and I spilt the salt when I was having breakfast, and whenever I do that something always happens. The last time I did it, I went out with a hole in my stocking.

CÆSAR. You should have thrown it three times over your left shoulder.

CLEOPATRA. I did.

CÆSAR. Then it's all right.

CLEOPATRA. No, it isn't, because as I did so I saw a single magpie in the garden and the gardener walked under a ladder and I noticed there were three lamps burning in the room.

CÆSAR. All right, I won't go.

CLEOPATRA. That's perfect.

CÆSAR. But on one condition.

CLEOPATRA. What is it ?

CÆSAR. That you put off Mark Antony to-night and dine with me instead.

CLEOPATRA. But, my dear Cæsar, it's impossible.

CÆSAR. Why ?

CLEOPATRA. Because I can't put off Mark Antony.

CÆSAR. Why not ?

CLEOPATRA. Well, because I never do put off people. Wait a second.

A slave brings in a letter

Someone has sent me an urgent letter. It's from Artemidorus. He says there's a plot. Wait——

OPERATOR. Three minutes.

CÆSAR *rings off and goes out*

CLEOPATRA *rings :*

CLEOPATRA. Is that the exchange ? Please put me on to Palatine, one four. We've been cut off ; no, not Palestine, Palatine. No, not a trunk call, *toll*. Palatine, Cæsar's house. Private line. . . .

OPERATOR. Sorry, there's no reply from Palatine one four.

CURTAIN